ANIMAL
RIGHTS
AND
HUMAN
WRONGS

ANIMAL RIGHTS AND HUMAN WRONGS

Sid Jenkins
with Michael Leitch

Lennard Publishing

LENNARD PUBLISHING
a division of Lennard Associates Ltd
Mackerye End
Harpenden
Herts AL5 5DR

British Library Cataloguing in Publication Data
is available

ISBN 1 85291 105 0

First published 1992

Cover design by Cooper Wilson
Editorial consultant Roderick Brown

Typeset in Palatino

Printed and bound in Great Britain
by Butler & Tanner Ltd, Frome and London

CONTENTS

CASEBOOK

APPENDIX

DEDICATION

This book is dedicated to Orlando,
the cat who has owned me for eleven years,
during which time he has been a constant
source of inspiration.

PREFACE

For 17 years I worked as a member of the Inspectorate of the RSPCA, and there was seldom a day when I did not witness some form of cruelty inflicted upon an animal by a human being.

During those 17 years I bottled up my feelings as I, along with others, battled to bring to justice those who caused such suffering, and struggled to educate the public about the basic rights of animals.

I also hid my frustration at the inability of the authorities to carry out their duties towards animals, as required by law. I felt that only by remaining patient could I achieve what was best for the animals I so strongly cared about.

No longer having to work within restraints I now take this opportunity to speak bluntly.

The words in this book are the words of an angry man. I make no apologies for them, and the reason I am angry is that even today, many forms of cruelty to animals persist unabated, despite the existence of legislation, sometimes over a century old, intended to prevent them.

Let's not beat about the bush: the way we care for animals in Britain is a shambles. Thanks to decades of neglect, deception and underfunding, we are in a state of crisis. Now there are fresh threats to be faced. These range from unsuitable laws which the European Parliament is seeking to impose on us, to the horrifying danger of infectious rabid animals entering Britain through the Channel Tunnel.

Unless we act soon, abandoning our Victorian system of amateur do-goodery in favour of a modern businesslike approach funded by Government money, the crisis will worsen, and the consequences will be explosive.

Drastic change is called for, and called for now: what we need is nothing less than a Minister for Animals heading a ministry with its own professional, publicly-funded Inspectorate. There should also be a complete re-drafting and up-dating of all our animal laws.

I invite you to read what I have to say. I hope you will agree that nothing less will do.

THE CASE
FOR CHANGE

ANIMAL RIGHTS AND HUMAN WRONGS

I believe that animals have natural rights. The most important of these is also the most fundamental: the right to exist freely alongside mankind on this planet which we all share. After all, in most cases, animals have been around a lot longer than we have.

I also believe that it is their natural right to live in the climate and environment of their native habitat, and that we humans have interfered with their natural lives by capturing them and taking them to other parts of our planet which are totally unsuitable for them.

Some animals we have confined to zoos and circuses, making them perform to provide us with pleasure. We have interfered with their natural rights to enjoy the space of their individual territories, the structure of their social orders and their natural feeding and breeding patterns; all things that they have in the wild and, of course, all things that we enjoy ourselves.

Other animals we have chosen to domesticate. These subservient animals rely on us to uphold their rights to exist in an environment that gives them adequate food, shelter and the opportunity to express their natural characteristics.

It might seem obvious to many reading this that animals *should* have natural rights. But for most of human history, animals had no rights at all. People were free to do with them exactly as they pleased. This situation was not just the result of ignorance or a lack of thought about the position of animals in the scheme of things: far from it. Philosophers have tried to place of animals within a coherent view of the world for at least two thousand years, giving widely differing results.

Writing before Christianity became the main code of thought for the western world, the Greek thinker Pythagoras, a vegetarian, taught that animals should be treated with respect, mainly because he believed that the souls of dead men migrated to animals. Aristotle, on the other hand, who believed in a strict hierarchy of society, and of all life, wrote that plants existed for the sake of animals, and animals for the sake of man, just as he believed that some kinds of men were inferior to others, and were thus fitted to be slaves. Neither philosophy shows concern for the rights of animals solely as animals.

Philosophers trying to find a place for animals within the teachings of Christianity produced a variety of theories, despite starting from a common source book, the Bible. St Augustine, writing in the fifth century AD, believed that Christ showed no particular concern for the rights of animals. When casting out the devils possessing a man in the country of the Gadarenes, Christ let them enter a herd of swine, which promptly ran over a cliff into the sea and drowned. The swine had not sinned in any way, and their fate in this incident led Augustine to pronounce that the codes of conduct which Christ taught us to apply to our behaviour towards our fellow men did not apply to our conduct towards animals. St Thomas Aquinas, who aimed to reconcile the teachings of pre-Christian philosophers with Christianity, concluded that man's behaviour towards animals was of no consequence since God had subjected all things to man's power, and although he also held that men should avoid cruelty towards animals in case such acts led to cruelty towards other men, Aquinas did not believe that cruelty towards animals should be avoided for the sake of the animals themselves.

Aquinas's views prevailed in many of the Church's subsequent rulings: in the nineteenth century, Pope Pius IX stopped the formation of a society to prevent cruelty to animals in Rome, as to allow such a body would be to accept that human beings had obligations towards animals.

Philosophers from the Renaissance onwards, liberated to some extent by a belief in humanism from the constraints of Christian teaching, rarely considered that animals had any place in the order of the world other than to serve man. A voice of dissent was heard from Michel de Montaigne who held that man's vanity led him to equal himself to God, and to separate himself from the 'crowd of other creatures'. Unfortunately teachings such as that of the French seventeenth-century thinker René Descartes held sway. Descartes believed that all creatures functioned according to the principles of mechanics, that is that they were machines. Man, uniquely, had a soul, specially created by God, which survived the destruction of the 'mechanical' body. Animals did not have souls, and as a result were devoid of consciousness. This view, which I find appalling, led to a further belief that every animal response, whether of pain, terror or need, was the result of a sophisticated kind of machinery invented by God, and did not indicate any feeling whatsoever. The disgusting results of this convenient theory were observed by Nicholas de Fontaine when he visited what would now be called 'research scientists' at Port-Royal in France, a prestigious seventeenth-century seat of learning:

'They administered beatings to dogs with perfect indifference, and made fun of those who pitied the creatures as if they felt pain. They said the animals were clocks; that the cries they emitted when struck were only the noise of a little spring that had been touched, but that the whole body was without feeling. They nailed poor animals up on boards by their four paws to vivisect them and see the circulation of the blood which was a great subject of conversation.'

I cannot forget this quotation. The way those people denied the existence of animal suffering goes against everything I have ever worked for. I agree completely with Voltaire, the eighteenth-century French thinker who, I believe, brilliantly refuted Descartes' theory:

'There are barbarians who seize this dog, who so greatly surpasses man in fidelity and friendship, and nail him down to a table and dissect him alive, to show you the mesaraic veins! You discover in him *all the same organs of feeling as in yourself*. Answer me, mechanist, has Nature arranged all the springs of feeling in this animal *to the end that he might not feel?*'

While I know that society, till at least the nineteenth century, was comparatively brutal – people were hanged for literally hundreds of offences which today we would punish with a suspended sentence, and slavery was practised in almost every nation – I still find it hard to accept that so many thinkers denied animals any real right to live their lives with dignity and without suffering. Take Immanuel Kant, writing in 1780:

'So far as animals are concerned, we have no direct duties.

Animals are not self-conscious, and are there merely as a means to an end. That end is man.'

This statement hardly hardly differs from the beliefs of Aristotle hundreds of years earlier. A fundamental change in public thinking was required before animals had any real rights at all, a change succintly pinpointed by Jeremy Bentham, the British philosopher, when considering the condition of animals, and the grounds for granting them rights: 'The question is not, Can they *reason*? nor Can they *talk*? but Can they *suffer*?'

This, I think, is an indication of the change in attitude that made it possible for some courageous MPs to propose the first bills designed to give animals the most basic of rights, enshrined in law. In 1821 Richard Martin proposed legislation intended to prevent ill-treatment of horses. This measure was received with dismissive laughter and derision, but Martin, determined to establish some basic protection for animals, persevered and due to his tenacity another bill making it an offence to mistreat certain domestic animals (excluding cats and dogs) became law in 1822.

Martin's legislation, properly titled The Act to Prevent the Cruel and Improper Treatment of Cattle, marked the beginning of a sequence of Acts of Parliament which, piecemeal, began to mean legally defined rights for animals, though initially only for certain animals and only in certain limited circumstances. As a result, animals have rights which have been gradually and rather clumsily established by Acts of Parliament. These certainly help, but we must never forget one essential fact. Animals depend totally on humans to help them.

Humans beings in trouble or distress, whatever their predicament, have organisations to which they can turn for help. They can contact one of many excellent helplines knowing that someone will be on the end of the line to offer support and comfort.

Animals cannot do this for themselves. Humans have to set up welfare services on their behalf, to deal with cases of individual hardship and to make sure that the laws made by Parliament to protect animals are respected and kept.

I repeat that we need more systematic legislation to protect all animals from human transgressors, because it is always people who cause the trouble to animals. When will more people realise that dogs and cats, all family pets, and all farm animals too, are helpless? All their lives they need protection, and the only person who can really give this to them is their owner. When he abuses this understanding, all hell breaks loose for the animal.

I never cease to be amazed by the diversity of 'crimes' committed against animals by mankind, a supposedly superior species. By crime, I mean any human act that leads to animal suffering. It should not be forgotten that it is just as much of a crime to neglect to care for an animal, which in legal terms is an act of omission, as it is to do actual harm, an act of commission.

I cannot hope to describe even one per cent of the atrocities that I have come across in my time. Instead I have selected a number of crimes to present in some detail. These crimes I have grouped together according to the type of human action responsible. I have chosen to start with cruelty, and the kinds of cruelty I write about will, I hope, appal you. I make no apologies for this. It's easy to be unaware of the scope of suffering inflicted on animals, and my intention here is to bring home to you, in the most effective way, the sorts of activity that we are up against. For several categories of crime, I also give a detailed account of a specific case that resulted in court proceedings under the heading 'Casebook', at the back of this book. The details are depressing and dispiriting, and reading them again I feel the rage I felt at the time, when pursuing the guilty parties. But only by giving you the blow-by-blow history of some of these cases can I communicate the cruelty, ignorance, selfishness and madness that threatens the right of all animals to a decent life.

I hope you will be shocked not only by these terrible crimes, but by the inadequate nature of current legislation (and its enforcement) which allows so many acts of cruelty, neglect and so on to occur. To make this crystal clear I outline the current state of animal legislation, and the hopeless system for implementing it, in the chapter entitled The Framework and The Flaws which follows my discussion of crimes against animals. It does not make happy reading. But it's my intention to show you just how drastic is the need for revision of the way animals' rights are safeguarded in this country. I offer my answers in the chapter after that: My Solutions. What I propose will not be easy: but there are no easy answers to abuses on such a grand scale. You may not agree with all I say: but at the very least, it's my aim to prove to you that something can, and must, be done.

CRUELTY

DOG-FIGHTING

NEILLSON v DREAD

Dread weighed in at 9.00 p.m. weight 75 lbs.
Neillson weighed in at 9.05 p.m. weight 48 lbs.
The fight started at 9.15 p.m.
Dread was top dog for 20 minutes.
Neillson took a leg hold.
First turn called at 30 minutes, two scratches each.
Neillson was picked up game at 47 minutes.
The fight finished at 10.02 p.m.
Owner of Neillson – Outlaw
Owner of Dread – Catch as Catch Can
Handler of Neillson – Bandit
Handler of Dread – Owner
Stakeholder – Dr Death
Referee – Mr. Inscape

In match reports the flesh-tearing obscenity of a pit bull terrier fight is carefully played down. Jargon and statistics are used to ritualise the action, and joke names obscure the identity of the principals.

The reality is very different – in no sense a ritual or a joke. The reality is horrific, vicious, lethal.

Consider the dogs. One look is enough to see that these are no casual street-fighters. They are purpose-bred, trained killers – low in build, heavily muscled in neck and shoulder, broad-headed ('brick-shaped' in the breed specification) with clipped ears and the meanest eyes of any breed.

Owners with pups to sell, or who offer their dog at stud, boast extensively about their animals' 'gameness', 'staying power', 'hard mouth', and so on. Here is a typical advertisement in *Pit Bull News*, the dog-fighters' underground magazine:

AT STUD. CH. SCOTSMANS MAX. £500. P.B.N. Dog of the Year 1986 and first official Champion. Four Outings – four wins. Twice approaching the 3 hour mark. "Max" has good air – durability and the *WILL TO WIN*. With 7 hours 45 minutes contract time to his credit "Max" has earned his reputation *the hard way* and is now enjoying a well deserved retirement.
Put to the right bitches, his offspring *must* stand a good chance. ENQUIRIES PLEASE RING, etc.

Advertisements are usually accompanied by the ludicrous claim: 'No dogs sold for illegal purposes.' Dog-fighting has been illegal since 1835.

The jaws of these animals are frightening. In training the owner hangs a padded bag or a car tyre from a rope attached to a tree branch. The dog springs up to it, the jaws lock on to the bag and the animal swings beneath, back legs paddling fiercely, well clear of the ground, while the owner shouts encouraging words: 'Good boy, Spike, good boy. Lock on. Shake it.'

These words are needless. The dog is so conditioned to not letting go, so tunnel-visioned in brute skills, that it can do nothing else but hang there and savage the training bag. When the owner decides the animal has done enough (up to 20 minutes is usual), there is no point in telling the dog to let go. The dog cannot, by itself, get loose from the bag. It has to be prised off with a breaking-stick, a chisel-ended piece of wood which is rammed in at the side of the dog's jaws and then turned to wrench the teeth apart. They use breaking-sticks in the pit bull arena, to separate the contestants. Imagine having teeth like that clamped onto your neck, or gnawing at your leg.

The fighting ring, or pit, has many shapes. Much depends on the venue and the scale of the occasion. Some fights in remote barns are attended by big crowds, the building carefully guarded by look-outs. Others take place in basements and cellars before a handful of spectators.

Some owners use house doors, placed on their side and fitted together to form a crude arena, about 14 feet square, its floor covered with a piece of carpet. The owners select a referee and timekeeper, and each appoints a handler and a chief second whose duty is to wash the opponent's dog before the fight and remain in that dog's corner as an observer.

The washing is done to make sure the dog has not been coated with a spray or some substance which the other dog could lick off and so choke or poison itself. Nice people you meet in the dog-fighting world – but a lot of money is at stake, so why should they trust each other?

When the washing is finished, each dog is towelled dry, wrapped in a blanket and carried to its corner by the handler. When both sides are ready, the referee calls, 'Face your dogs'.

The handlers place the dogs in front of a scratch-line – a tape or painted line near each corner – and on the command 'Let go', the dogs are released and must start across the line towards their opponent.

The fight is a grinding battle of attrition. Rules and procedures vary from place to place, but the essentials are always the same. The two dogs clash, each seeking a hold, usually on the jaw or neck. The teeth close and the animals push and maul like front-row forwards in an everlasting scrum.

This is where hard training on the treadmill pays off. In preparation for a fight, the dogs are made to practise for hours inside a cage with a moving floor, building up stamina and power in their legs and thighs. As an inducement to keep his animal running, the owner may get a live cat or bird and hold it in front of the dog, just out of reach. When the session is over he gives it to the dog.

There is another sickening aspect to training a dog for combat; other dogs are needed. The owner may have an 'old pro' dog in his kennels, what they call a 'sparring partner' – a bit slow and rickety but skilled enough to teach the younger dog how to move in and get a hold without exposing itself.

The trainers then put the novice dog in with a 'taste dog' – literally, an animal taken off the streets to have the flesh torn from it. Sometimes, 'target' areas of its body are shaved, to show the young dog which parts to attack. After a few 'real mouthfuls' the new dog needs little encouragement.

In most fights, the first 15 or 20 minutes are a long desperate clinch. This is the time for the slow breaking-down of the opponent. One of them must eventually give ground, its spirit broken by that crucial fraction which makes the difference between winners and losers.

The handlers urge them on, crouching and kneeling beside them. 'Good lad, good lad. Shake 'im.' Blood begins to run from a torn mouth or neck, coating the pit walls with dark orange smears.

The dogs fight on, sometimes with muffled growls and snarls, but for much of the time in menacing silence, broken at last by cries of pain as one dog weakens. The handlers watch keenly. Will it turn? This is critical. If, under modern rules, a dog turns its head, shoulders and front feet away from the opponent, the referee can order both dogs to be picked up. Breaking-sticks may be needed to prise them apart, but they must be separated. Then the handlers take them back to their corners, and the dog which 'turned' must now prove its gameness by 'scratching'.

After an interval of 30 seconds, the timekeeper calls out 'Let go', and the dog, now faced towards its opponent, must start instantly over its scratch-line and get across to the other dog without stopping or hesitating. The fight is joined again. 'Turns' and 'scratches' follow each other until one dog fails to make its scratch and is declared the loser.

It takes a long time to wear one of these four-legged bruisers into submission. They are trained for battles lasting an hour or more, and have immense natural strength. To the pride of its owner, a good dog exhibits unquestioning courage, and what are called 'fine sporting qualities'. It is expected to do this whether winner or loser, and regardless of injuries.

Naturally, however, no-one wants to be lumbered with a losing dog. So, to push the odds in their favour, the owners drug their animals. Before the fight, a dose of Azium is injected. Used legitimately by vets, this drug is intending for treating inflammation and shock. Used by the pit bull cowboys, it keeps a dog on its feet, up and scratching, when it is really half-dead or worse. They get the drugs from various illicit sources, including the self-styled 'experts' who travel hundreds of miles on the dog circuit to patch up dogs, and who have access to drugs.

Most fights do not end with a death. These dogs are too expensive to chuck away that fast – owners will have paid between

£250 and £500 for a high-class pup. From the owner's point of view, it is better to pick up a dog which clearly no longer has a chance of winning. Then they take it home, call in the medical 'expert' or do the patching up themselves – they can't consult a licensed vet unless they know a bent one. Then they put the dog back in training and hope for better luck next time out.

After a fight both dogs are exhausted, desperately tired. If the loser is lucky it lies on its side, tongue out, battling to regain its breath like an athlete after a gruelling race. It will have nasty cuts on the body but the drugs help it to combat them. In a few minutes it will get to its feet and be ready to leave the venue.

The *unlucky* loser will be far worse off. The injuries will be horrific – a gaping wound in the head or a leg torn off. I have seen wounds so terrible that any sane person would be nauseated by them. So what does that make the owners, who allow such suffering to happen to their own dog – and do so in the name of sport?

They are sick, these people, there can be no doubt about it – failures in life who have resorted to dog-fighting to jack up their flagging self-esteem. Many have records of domestic and criminal violence.

To see the other side of this, you only have to look at the owner of the winning dog. A 'game' dog, particularly one which is successful in the pit and brings in the money, is idolised by its owner. The owner takes the dog down to the local pub where pit bull fanatics gather, and shows it off to anyone who will listen. If his macho pride needs further bolstering, and it usually does, he will make sure a match report is sent off to *Pit Bull News*, which in Britain has cornered the market in this most shameful of sports. He may even submit a poem about it, as the owner did in the casebook story I describe later in this book.

He may have his animal photographed, pin-up style, leaning forward on a taut leash and wearing a thick studded collar or 'breast-plate' harness. He may even have his champion painted in oils – the service is advertised in *Pit Bull News*.

He will certainly want to make the most of the dog's earnings potential by putting it out to stud. At £250 to £500 a time, it's a lot better than working for the money.

And when the dog dies, especially if it's a premature death, he will weep, and maybe write a maudlin obituary to be published in, where else, *Pit Bull News*. Below is the last word on Smuggler, a so-called champion, as it appeared in the magazine.

CH. SMUGGLER
Ch. "Smuggler" born – November 1983. Deceased – Oct. 1986

It was my privilege and pleasure to know this dog during his short lifetime. He was to my mind a great little Bulldog who I am sure would have gone on to win his Gr. Ch. but for a tragic accident which cost him his life.

He was what all Bulldog men love to see, an "early-starter", at the tender age of 6 weeks he was "hot-to-go", and had to be separated from his litter mates. In fact most of the litter had this tendency and were separated accordingly. He was a dream dog to condition and worked with an intensity that had to be seen to be believed! He had natural wind, and you could take him off the chain, and he would run a mill flat-out for $^1/_2$ hour or more before slowing down! During his last "keep" I went to see my good friend V.E. who was "working" him for his Championship match, which was a week away. V.E. was bringing him to a "peak" and at this stage his roadwork was up to 20 miles followed by $2^1/_2$ hours millwork – such was his capacity for work.

His Championship was won in fairly short order, none of his opponents taking him beyond the hour. He was a great pit-general who could pace himself, and pour on the pressure when necessary. He was not a good "biter" but his love for fighting made up for that. He was the type of dog you would say is "game" although he never had to show "gameness" in any of his contests, you just knew by the burning in his eyes he would go "all-the-way". He never made one bad sign in his life – a real "man's-dog". You knew if you went inside his chain that he had respect for you, and would let you "pet" him.

Many first class dogmen in this country had the pleasure of seeing this little fellow in action, and they will tell you that he was a good honest Bulldog that you would love to own. I believe he was bred to a few good females and there are pups around from him. I hope one or two carry on their father's name to where he loved to be "in-the-pit".

Here's to you "Smuggler"
A great little Bulldog.

Dirty Harry.

Smuggler was in fact put down after inflicting head injuries on the six-year-old daughter of its new owner.

Not all dogs end up winners, of course, and naturally there are limits to the patience of a losing owner. Losses hit both his pride and his pocket. There are expressions for a dog which won't fight properly. They are called a 'cur', which means a coward. If a dog is declared 'curred out' at the end of a fight, this reflects badly on the owner. A dog with no bottle is no use to him.

Then there is the money. Each time the dog is beaten, the owner loses his stake money. This is seldom less than £200, and may be much more, so a useless dog will have to go. Here again there is a problem. He cannot just hand the animal over to the RSPCA or a vet, to be put down or found a new home. The dog's scars will betray its illegal fighting career, and that could bring trouble with the law. As often as not, the dog is killed at the owner's home, its body stuck in a bin-liner and taken down the tip, or dumped over some railway embankment.

So much for friendship, for the trust between a man and the animal he kept as his so-called pet.

From Bulldog to Pit Bull: The History of Dog-fighting
I have gone at some length into the details of what happens at an organised dog-fight for several reasons. I wanted, first of all, to point out its gruesome nature and the cruelty invariably suffered by the dogs.

They are powerless, remember. A man, for reasons of background, physique or whatever, may grow up a fighter, and then want to prove himself either in the ring or on the streets. The choice to do so is his alone. A dog, however, has no such choice. A dog is always the victim – bred, trained and compelled to fight at the whim of an owner.

Dog-fighting is a worldwide scandal. Among our European neighbours, it flourishes as an underground activity in Ireland, Belgium and Holland. Across the Atlantic it is widespread in the United States, Canada and Mexico. It certainly has a following in Japan and no doubt is practised in other Far Eastern countries. What we are really addressing is an international racket which has deep roots in many of our older civilisations and has since been taken up with enthusiasm in other, more recently developed lands.

In England, animal baiting has a long history. The baiting of bulls and bears by dogs was common in the Middle Ages, but, by the eighteenth century, spectacles involving the public torture of bulls and bears had lost the mass appeal they once had. Instead, the owners of bulldogs, formerly used for baiting bulls, began to match their dogs against each other. There had been dog-fighting before, but now it became fashionable. It shared with cock-fighting the advantage that it was cheap to organise and could be put on at small venues such as a stable yard or the back room of a public house. Dog-fighting drew working men in steady numbers, plus a regular sprinkling of upper- and middle-class visitors. The appeal was crude but effective: a night out drinking, a few laughs, and live entertainment that spectators could lay bets on and maybe win a few shillings.

For some while, the bulldog remained the ideal fighting dog. Its courage and tenacity were legendary, its great strength beyond doubt. As John Bull's chosen dog, it even became a national emblem, promoted in the *Punch* cartoons of Sir John Tenniel and John Leech. However, it was never the most agile of breeds and owners began to look for a dog that would be less ponderous in the pit, a dog that would be fast on the turn without any loss of shoving power, grip and stamina.

Breeders began to cross their animals with Old English terriers, and this gave them a more satisfactory fighting dog. Known for a time as 'the bull and the terrier', then as a 'bull terrier', the type reached its high point in the county of Staffordshire.

This is not to say that the Staffordshire bull terrier evolved primarily as a fighting dog. It first appeared as a distinct breed around 1870 (and was not recognised as such by the Kennel Club until 1935). It could not have become established without the efforts of a long line of conscientious, legitimate dog-breeders. Today it is widely valued as a tough, loyal and affectionate pet – though would-be buyers are usually, and should *always*, be warned that it is dangerous to take on a Staffordshire unless they are prepared to train it strictly, especially in restraint towards other dogs.

It is only a ruthless minority who have spoiled the reputation of the breed. They recognised the extraordinary power of these dogs, and then sought to exploit them and so create the most effective fighting machine in the canine world.

By the time the Staffordshire bull terrier emerged as a separate breed, dog-fighting had been outlawed in Britain. This was due to an Act of Parliament passed in 1835, which also banned the baiting of bulls and bears, and cock-fighting. But when Queen Victoria began her reign, two years later, dog-fighting and cock-fighting were still popular forms of amusement, despite this legislation. Organisers of these sports merely went underground, and have been there ever since.

The rise of the American Pit Bull Terrier
Some time after the American Civil War, emigrants to the United States began taking their dogs with them to start a new life together. Some of these were fighting dogs of the bull terrier type. The breed became popular and more were sent for. From them gradually appeared the new breed known today as the American pit bull terrier.

This is a larger dog than the English original, and shares all its characteristics of strength and tenacity. According to the United Kennel Club, set up in 1898 in order to register pit bulls in America, dogs do not have to conform to rigid standards, since they are bred as performance animals and not for show. Colour, weight, nose colour and colour of eyes are thus not seen as important, though as a general guide the preferred weight for dogs is 35-60 lb and for bitches 30-50 lb.

Since its establishment in the United States, the American pit bull terrier has taken over as the most popular type of fighting dog. They are now bred throughout Britain (although recent legislation, namely the Dangerous Dogs Act 1991, Section 2 (a), makes it an offence to breed, or breed from, any dog of the type known as the pit bull terrier) and on the Continent, and they are widely admired. Some American pit bull terriers may have Staffordshire blood in them, for some breeders think the pure-bred English dog has a harder bite.

The Staffordshire and the American pit bull terrier are far and away the most ferocious and successful fighting breeds. At various times there have been trial matches between pit bulls and other dogs thought to have the requisite qualities, but invariably the pit bull wins. Rottweilers, Bullmastiffs and Giant Schnauzers are quickly worn down and badly beaten.

An American writer has summarised it like this: 'When a pit man says that a pit dog can demolish any member of any other breed, he doesn't mean maybe.'

The same writer added: 'Pit fights are also occasionally staged between pit dogs and an absolutely startling number of wild animals, such as wolverines, wolves, badgers, raccoons and even baboons ... in *all* of the above cases a pit dog must be smaller (spot weight) than any of these animals in order for the wild animal to stand a chance.'

Cruelty from the nineteenth century
The dog-fighting fanatics know the dogs suffer – they have to attend to their wounds after a fight – but their selfishness overrides any compassion. They will even use history to justify what they do. 'I know it's a bit cruel,' runs the argument, 'but it's always gone on, hasn't it?'

This, to their lazy minds, is enough to justify the suffering of the animals. And there must always be suffering, because without the blood, pain and damage, the whole structure of dog-fighting would immediately collapse.

Unfortunately, the words of Henry Mayhew, whose *London Labour and the London Poor* was first published in 1851, still apply to some people:

'Home has few attractions to a man whose life is a street-life. Even those who are influenced by family ties and affections, prefer to 'home' – indeed that word is rarely mentioned among them – the conversation, warmth, and merriment of the beer-shop, where they can take their ease among their mates. *Excitement or amusement are indispensable to uneducated men.'* [my italics]

It is not appropriate in this book to enter into a discussion about work, wages and leisure in Victorian England, except perhaps to say that the vast majority of people today enjoy a much freer and more civilised lifestyle. It is, however, fitting to examine the similarities between dog-fighting then and now. Take away some modern technology, (though not much more than the use of electricity), and the two worlds – of 1851 and 1992– are shockingly alike.

Writing specifically about costermongers (in his context they were street-sellers of fish, fruit and vegetables), Mayhew states: 'Their dog-fights are both cruel and frequent. It is not uncommon to see a lad walking with the trembling legs of a dog shivering under a bloody handkerchief, that covers the bitten and wounded body of an animal that has been figuring at some "match". These fights take place on the sly – the tap-room or back-yard of a beer-shop, being generally chosen for the purpose. A few men are let into the secret, and they attend to bet upon the winner, the police being carefully kept from the spot.'

Elsewhere in his book, an informant describes to Mayhew 'the order of the combat':

'We'll say now that it's a scratch fight; two dogs each have their corner of a pit, and they're set to fight. They'll fight on till they go down together, and then if one leaves hold, he's sponged. Then they fight again. If a dog has the worst of it he mustn't be picked up, but if he gets into his corner, then he can stay for as long as may be agreed upon, minute or half-minute time, or more than a minute. If a dog won't go to the scratch out of his corner, he loses the fight. If they fight on, to settle it, one must be killed – though that very seldom happens, for if a dog's very much punished, he creeps to his corner and don't come out to time, and so the fight's settled. Sometimes it's agreed beforehand, that the master of a dog may give in for him; sometimes that isn't to be allowed ...'

This is a remarkable testament. It shows that the rules and practices of dog-fighting, as carried out today, were already laid down and in place more than 140 years ago. The scratches, the washing, the rules about refusing to fight, winning and losing – all are virtually identical with modern rules.

It is even more remarkable when you think that the basics of all our major above-the-board sports – cricket, rugby, soccer, and so on – were still in a relatively undeveloped state. It certainly says little for the social and mental advancement of the dog-fighters that they have turned their backs on progress for such a huge span of time.

The menace to society

Make no mistake, these men are dangerous. They constantly steal and maim each other's dogs, and feud and fight among themselves. Three incidents in recent years attest to their extreme violence. A pit bull owner was shot through the head at his flat in Shoreditch, East London. He had no criminal connections apart from his links with the dog pits. In Merseyside a man with dog-fighting connections had his arm severed in an 'accident'.

These incidents were unsolved. The pit bull men closed ranks. No-one squealed. More perturbing is the fact that their violence extends beyond their immediate world, affecting neighbours and the innocent public as a whole. Get too close to these men, however innocently, and you risk being shot. Incidents involving shotguns and crossbows are well documented.

And the stealing of family pets still goes on. Next time, it may be your dog, or a dog in your street, particularly if it is a bull terrier or some other reputedly aggressive breed. In a typical recent incident Lucy, a two-year-old Staffordshire bull terrier, vanished from outside the home of her owners, near Bradford.

Lucy was no fighting dog, just a family pet. She was found four days later, where she had been dumped, needing more than 20 stitches in deep cuts to her head and chest. The vet who examined her had little doubt that the wounds were from fighting injuries.

We are now up to date, or nearly so. I have described the background to dog-fighting, and what actually happens at a fight. It is time to look briefly at the legal position and at the reasons why, for so long, bodies such as the RSPCA could make so little progress in their efforts to stamp out these horrific practices.

Legal loopholes

Until well into the 1980s, there was a massive gap between what I and my colleagues in the RSPCA Inspectorate wanted to do, and what we could actually achieve. We had long felt it should be a top-priority issue to bring to justice and secure heavy punishments for anyone who either fights or baits any kind of animal. We were united in our contempt for these sadists.

My view at the time, which I stick to, was that there should be an automatic prison sentence for all convicted of participation in these activities, whether as an owner, referee or merely as a spectator. The animals involved would be confiscated and all those found guilty would be disqualified for life from keeping any animal.

However, as the law stood, we would get nowhere unless we could raid a fight and catch the people red-handed. Arriving either before or afterwards was useless. We might be able to secure minor prosecutions under the 1911 Protection of Animals Act for example, for failing to provide necessary care and attention for a pit bull dog which was clearly suffering from wounds obtained in a fight. But the penalties were far too slight. A fine, coupled with a ban, might be all we could get, and that might be limited to one offender only. To make any impression on the dog-fighting racket as a whole, we needed more comprehensive legislation and more severe penalties.

In 1989 we at last made a breakthrough in the case described at the back of this book. It happened in my area in the North-East of England. Ironically, when we began our investigations, we had no idea we would get so far. Following that case, and other attacks by pit bull dogs, in particular on six-year-old Rukshana Khan in Bradford, the Government hurriedly introduced legislation in the form of the Dangerous Dogs Act of 1991. This act in my opinion was ill-conceived, and subsequent court cases, resulting in the dismissal of summonses, have proved the act to be unworkable. Little Rukshana lived: others did not.

BADGER-BAITING

I have an RSPCA certificate of commendation in my office. Usually you feel a little proud if your Headquarters wants to commemorate something you did while carrying out your everyday duties. Not on this occasion. Remembering how I earned this award gives me no pleasure at all. I will go further: the thought of it makes me sick.

A man came to us, to ask if we could rescue his dog. He told us that the last time he had seen his dog was when he was out taking his child for a walk. They had reached a field, then the dog had run off and gone underground after a rabbit. He had tried to call him back but had not heard or seen any sign of the animal since then.

He offered to take me to the spot and I went with him. The hole was above a known badger sett, and it was clear to me that this man had put his dog down the hole to try and flush out a badger. Then somehow the dog had become trapped below ground.

We mounted a rescue operation which received wide publicity. The press and television were there. We used every device we could think of to try and make contact with the dog and we even had an ultrasound detector to pick up any faint noise the dog might make. All in vain. For all we knew, the dog could have died within minutes of going underground into a maze of tunnels and chambers.

The owner, meanwhile, played up to the press attention. He did seem genuinely upset at losing his dog. All through the search, he claimed he knew nothing about badgers. The dog had bolted, he said. It had just run off and gone down the hole. I found it impossible to sympathise with him. I knew he was lying, and that he had put the dog in there himself. If we had been able to obtain proof of this, I would gladly have seen him prosecuted for causing unnecessary suffering to the animal.

We finally abandoned the search on the advice of mining engineers who said that if we dug any further, the embankment would collapse. It appeared that the dog was dead, and so the owner agreed that no more could be done. I gave the order to stop up the hole to save it from further suffering and so the dog was buried – alive or dead. It was a very depressed group of men that finally left the scene. The nagging doubt that the dog might still be alive bore heavily on us all.

Among British mammals the badger occupies a strange and precarious position. About 250,000 live beneath our countryside, for the most part in open, deciduous woodlands. They are shy, gentle, nocturnal. They do little harm to anyone, and few farmers object to them. They eat a variety of foods including earthworms, beetles and fruit. They are relatively large-bodied, weighing up to 50lb (22kg), and belong to the *Mustelidae*, or musk-bearing family, along with stoats, weasels, otters, martens and other animals.

When seen, they are unmistakeable. The long-snouted black and white striped face is universally known and recognised. Any child can tell you what a badger looks like; very few will have seen one, except in pictures.

The same goes for adults. Perhaps it is the badger's elusiveness which explains why so many men are obsessed with hunting it, digging it up and destroying it. Each year, diggers and baiters cause some 9,000 badgers to die – after prolonged terrorising and torture. They call it sport, but it is nothing less than a massacre.

This one-sided war between the badger and its persecutors has been going on for hundreds of years. In medieval society the badger, the bear and the bull were the favoured baiting animals, set upon by dogs which wore them down and prepared them for slaughter at the climax of the ritual.

Under the Badgers Act 1973 and the Wildlife and Countryside Acts of 1981 and 1985, it is illegal for any person to kill, injure or take a badger. There are bans on the use of gas, poison and snares for trapping badgers, and it is also illegal to possess a dead badger or even a pelt taken from a dead animal. No one may keep, sell or try to sell a live badger, or mark or ring one. Offenders face prison sentences of up to three months, and fines of up to £2,000.

Still the war goes on, despite the efforts of the police, and various volunteer groups which have formed all over the country to monitor and protect the local setts. In some places, the badger has come close to extinction. In the Rotherham area, part of the territory covered by the South Yorkshire Badger Group, a survey showed that between 1977 and 1985, sett numbers fell from 40 to four. Nearly all of these losses were attributed to a demented gang of diggers who lived in Rotherham and in nearby villages.

Since the intervention of the South Yorkshire Badger Group, the number of setts near Rotherham has increased to 16, and in the group's whole territory there are now 200 active setts.

But what an intervention it was. In order to save their badgers, the volunteers dug large shallow holes a foot deep above the setts, inserted sheets of steel mesh wired together and pinned with spikes, then poured a layer of concrete onto the mesh. Then they raked back the soil and covered it with turf and leaves until no sign was left to tell that they had been there.

The badgers now had a roof as secure as an air-raid bunker. When the diggers next paid a night-time call, their spades hit concrete and they went off empty-handed. Slowly the badger community began to restore itself, helped also by artificial setts made of breeze blocks and pipes which were sunk deep into the ground and left for badgers to occupy. Local firms donated materials and Rotherham District Council loaned construction workers to install the mesh and concrete roofs.

It is a most impressive scheme, and I congratulate all those involved. What a pity, though, that such massive ingenuity had to be brought to bear to save a community of harmless badgers.

Their tormentors fall into two groups – the diggers and the baiters. In some areas they work together, or are one and the same group. The main distinction is that the diggers are the providers. They locate and capture badgers and may then sell them on to a gang of baiters, who then use dogs to kill them off. For some diggers the hunt is an end in itself, and they kill the badger soon after it is hauled from the sett. Many others, though, are mindful of the money to be earned – upwards of £300 – by supplying a live badger for an organised 'do' or 'bait' as it is called.

The diggers work either in secret at dead of night, or they con a farmer into letting them onto his land with an offer to get rid of his rabbits or foxes. Their method is to locate the entrance to a sett, then send down a dog, usually some kind of terrier or working dog, which chases and traps the badger. The dog may carry an electronic tag around its neck, so the diggers can pinpoint its position below ground with a responding device. Then they dig down to the badger and catch it in a net.

The 'bait' is the killing ritual. The organiser appoints the time and place, and invites a number of dog owners and gambling spectators to attend. The dogs are set on the badger one at a time, and the spectators bet among themselves on how long the badger will last, in minutes and seconds. When the badger is weakened to a point where it cannot protect itself, time is called and the badger is killed off. 'Spading it' is the casual term these people use, meaning that the badger is smashed over the head with a spade.

In a one-to-one fight, a badger makes a formidable opponent. They are tough animals, bite back fiercely, and when crouched in a defensive position offer little for the dog to get hold of. Fighting dogs are trained to go for the scruff of an opponent, then lock on and shake until the badger is worn out. At a badger-bait it may take several dogs to weaken the badger, or the organiser may throw in more than one dog at a time. The result is always the same: the badger is terrorised and suffers a drawn-out, agonising death.

The case study later in this book, a typical example of a badger dig, resulted in prison sentences and fines for two of the offenders and a fine for a third man. In this instance justice was seen to be done, even though the sentences were reduced on appeal.

It is difficult, except in one respect, to see how the law might be improved in relation to badger digging and baiting. If there were more time, and more people available – as there would be if we had a proper Government Inspectorate – it would be possible to set up a nationwide monitoring scheme, using the existing volunteer forces and building on them, to protect the badger population *as a whole*. That would provide a much better base from which to administer the law.

Meanwhile I believe the law should be adjusted to make it an offence to dig or disturb the ground above a known badger sett. By protecting the sett as well as the badgers, we would deny offenders the chance to employ their most commonly used excuse – that they were looking for rabbits or foxes, not badgers. Too many offenders swing this plea on lenient magistrates and get away with it. We need to close this loophole without delay.

The remaining task is not so simple. It is to devise ways to deter the diggers and baiters from carrying on their barbaric activities. They work mainly in local groups, some of which are connected through the marketing activities of certain diggers. An effective digger may in fact have a wide range of contacts who get in touch with him when they want to stage a bait and require another badger. Basically, however, the men who persecute these fascinating animals are isolated groups of misguided individuals.

Although we need to remain as vigilant as ever, and enforce the law whenever possible, I believe the long-term answer lies in education, in persuading future generations of youngsters that the badger deserves more respect than we have given it in the past. The badger thrives on a nocturnal and private form of existence. It cannot change its ways, and we should be content to let it be.

Anyone who really wants to see and learn about badgers should join a local monitoring group. They aim not just to protect badgers from criminal intruders. On a much more positive level, they locate and record the setts in their area, and monitor and survey badgers in their habitat. Most provide a general education service to the public and carry out studies for the public and private bodies that approach them. By joining a group, a newcomer would have an incomparable opportunity to observe badgers and gain some precious understanding of how they go about their daily lives. That is what I call a real challenge: the chance to acquire knowledge about one of our most misunderstood animals.

COCK-FIGHTING AND QUAIL-FIGHTING

Cock-fighting has long been shunned by the Western world. In Britain it has been illegal since 1835, and if it can be said to flourish anywhere it does so only in primitive, underdeveloped areas of Mexico, Haiti and Puerto Rico.

In England it was part of a robust, somewhat benighted culture which saw nothing wrong in using animal fights and baits as vehicles for gambling. All classes joined in. When Samuel Pepys went to a cockpit in 1663 he reported seeing everyone from 'parliament men' to 'the poorest prentices, bakers, brewers, butchers, draymen and what not ... all fellows one with another in swearing, cursing and betting'. The diarist's own frank view of animal sports was that they gave him 'a very rude and nasty pleasure'.

At that time the mass of the population did not see cruelty in the way we understand it today. There was a huge indifference to the fate of animals, and boys freely terrorised all kinds of creatures. They robbed birds' nests, hunted squirrels, tied bottles and cans to dogs' tails, dropped cats from tall buildings, cut off pigs' tails and inflated frogs' bodies by blowing into them with a straw. At country fairs people competed at biting off the heads of live chickens and sparrows. Another cruel sport was cock-throwing, in which the bird was tethered to a stake or buried up to its neck, and boys threw sticks at it until they killed it.

In modern times cock-fights are fairly rare, and difficult to anticipate or track down. They take place in remote country yards or where travellers gather, and are essentially private, clannish occasions. There is betting on the outcome of a fight, but further information about this activity is hard to come by.

There is also an ethnic variation, introduced to Britain by immigrants from Pakistan. The animal they use is the Asiatic quail. It is a small bird, little bigger than a starling. In preparation for a fight, the handlers sharpen the bird's beak and claws with a razor blade. They paint the talons red and feed the animal with a mash or bran steeped in alcohol to arouse its fighting nature.

The organisers operate extensive rings. I know that in West Yorkshire they are active in Bradford, Leeds and Halifax. Fights are held in cellars and remote barns and attract big crowds, summoned by telephone at short notice. Certain taxi firms are in on the racket and convey passengers to the fights.

The quails, usually cock-birds, are pitted against each other in 10-minute bouts. They are fierce fighters and can kill an opponent in that space of time. Not many fights go to the death, but the birds inflict terrible injuries on each other.

The main purpose of a quail-fight is to provide an arena where massive sums of money can be staked. Thousands of pounds change hands in bets at some bouts.

Efforts to pin down the fighting rings have had limited success. The gangs are elusive and scatter quickly at the first sign of a raid. After one near-miss valuable photographic evidence was obtained which revealed much about the fights and the state of the birds which were coerced into taking part. I hope it will not be too long before quail-fighting is stamped out completely.

DOMESTIC VIOLENCE

Cases of cruelty to a family pet are all the more sad when the animal is the victim of sudden or premeditated violence. Out of the blue, someone – a person the animal may have known and trusted – attacks it, and the animal's life is ended, or horribly changed.

Why do these things happen? First of all, I should make it clear I am referring to a particular category of abuse which, though not an everyday occurrence, happens often enough. It is also by its very nature domestic, for like so many human assault and murder cases, it has its roots in the home.

A couple fall out, and the pet is selected by one of them for an act of vengeance. Maybe it was the woman's cat, and the man wants to get back at her. Or a father cannot stand losing authority over a grown-up son or daughter, and directs his rage at the child's favourite animal. This was the problem that led to the dreadful case given at the back of this book.

The permutations are many. Usually the offender is male, and middle-aged or older. Women seldom commit these sudden acts of revenge, nor do young people.

I also include in this category violence committed by a neighbour. In my experience, the jealousy and hatred aroused by the habits of people living next door can be as volcanic and painful as the tension generated within the four walls of home.

One day the lid flies off. It only takes one fit of uncontrolled temper, a spasm lasting just a few minutes after maybe years of uneasy peace, but the effects can be deadly. Take the example of a case I dealt with in Leeds:

There was a long-running quarrel between two families living next door to one another. It had gone on for years, but suddenly reached boiling point when one man attacked two of his neighbours' dogs with a sharp instrument, believed to be a scythe, leading to wounds that needed surgery and stitching. The quarrel still continued in the street with the man wielding an axe in public. He was then arrested by the police.

In court the assailant was found guilty of causing unnecessary suffering to the dogs and was fined £200 with £50 costs. He and his wife, and their neighbours, a mother and son, were all bound over to keep the peace for two years. At least these dogs survived, though badly injured in the mindless attack.

One of the worst aspects of this type of abuse is that we can do nothing to prevent any particular outburst. I found that when I arrived on the scene, summoned by the police or a distressed member of the family, the damage had been done – revenge had been exacted. A lifeless body lay stretched on the floor.

Here is another case in which the animal was simply the victim of human passions. Rather than meet the responsibilities of taking Duke, a six-year-old black and tan dog, for a walk, his owner just turned him out to 'go' on his own. Duke made his way to the garden of a nearby house, no doubt lured by the scent of the bitch that lived there who was on heat. The owner of the bitch, fed up with the number of dogs visiting his garden, finally lost control, took his air rifle and shot Duke in the neck. Duke staggered home and died in his owner's arms. The 25-year-old man was taken to court and charged with 'causing unnecessary suffering to a dog by wantonly shooting and wounding'. He was fined £50 and ordered to pay £200 costs. But if Duke's owner had faced up to his responsibility, none of this would have happened.

I used to find it difficult not to feel anger at such moments. It was not just the dreadful waste of a life, or the renewing of the knowledge that people were capable of such senseless violence; it was also a response to the plight of domestic animals everywhere that provoked my feelings. Animals are so helpless. They depend on their owners for love and kindness, as well as for food and shelter, and can do nothing against this kind of attack. Like a child, they have no chance of escape.

Then the demands of routine would take over. My job became that of an investigator, piecing together the story of what had happened from all the evidence. Maybe nothing could be done to help this animal, but for the sake of all family pets, the offender had to be found and prosecuted.

In the beginning, oddly enough, it might not be obvious who was responsible. The guilty person might be right there in the room, but might be unwilling to admit what had been done. He might try to reject what had really happened, pushing it out of mind; he might even flatly deny having had any part in it.

It would sometimes take hours of detective work to obtain enough evidence with which to confront the offender with the intention of prompting a confession from him. Faced with a refusal to confess, I would do my best to pick holes in his story – a flawed alibi maybe, or something that connected him to the weapon used, despite denials of such a connection. In this way I would try to let him see that I already knew more than he was prepared to admit.

Then he might weaken. He might feel suddenly driven to bluff his way out of the corner. He might start shouting that I would never be able to prove it in court. When I heard those words, I knew it would not be long before I learned the whole truth.

THOSE WHO KILL FOR CONVENIENCE

This is the most unpleasant group of all offenders. Their actions prove how totally unsuited they are to keeping any kind of animal.

There can be no excuses. Drunkenness is often a factor, but cannot be used to mitigate killing or badly injuring a family pet. These people take on an animal, usually a dog, then find that they cannot cope with its needs. A bitch cries to be with her puppies, and in effect signs her own death warrant. Puppies turn out to be too boisterous for their owners' liking, and are disposed of in the crudest possible manner. I'd like to give you just one example, which I'm afraid is all too typical of the suffering inflicted on animals.

Kicking two young puppies to death led to a 37-year-old unemployed man being sent to prison for 30 days. It also led to his being banned from keeping any animal for the rest of his life. The woman with whom he was living was fined £100 and banned from keeping animals for the rest of her life, after admitting two charges of causing unnecessary suffering by allowing the animals to be killed in an improper manner.

The presiding Magistrate told the man, 'We hear you are disgusted with yourself. We are disgusted with you. You kicked those little animals to death.' Turning to address the woman, the Magistrate said, 'Your solicitor has asked for mercy on your behalf; you showed these dogs no mercy.'

The reasons the couple gave for kicking the dogs to death was that they had become too much trouble for the woman to look after and the man did not like them. This, they thought, was sufficient reason for killing the puppies in an appalling and cruel way.

When such people are convicted, the magistrates impose life bans and occasionally a prison sentence. There is nothing more they can do. The convictions are occasionally accompanied by garish accounts in the local newspapers but very rarely do these cases get the publicity they rightly deserve. Stories about neighbours in disgrace always have an irresistible appeal to readers. I just hope that they carry the right message and successfully deter others from committing similar crimes; and that younger readers feel a proper revulsion, which they will remember and learn from.

This type of violence is a problem that society as a whole must grapple with and try to cure. Try as we might, with educational programmes, school visits and so on, society seems powerless to deal with that sinister violent streak which in some people surfaces with fatal effect for animals.

Perhaps we should be thankful for the progress that has been made in the last few years. In the days of my childhood it was common to dispose of unwanted puppies and kittens by drowning them in a bucket. Thank goodness those days are over. It does still happen, but I do think there has been a change for the better in our sympathy and respect for animals. Long may that continue.

BLAMING THE ANIMAL FOR OUR FAILINGS

Competing in events can bring out the worst in us. When we compete, it can be a case of win at all costs, and when things go wrong when animals are involved, they often carry the blame for human error – from the shepherd who gives the wrong command at sheepdog trials to the owner of the dog at agility tests, who gets over excited and sends the dog over the wrong obstacle. But, for me, the worst are a small minority of the showjumping fraternity.

Here we pass to the wealthier class of owner. Usually it is the daughter's pony, and usually it is Daddy who does the paying. The family has somewhere to keep the pony, and they can afford to join the Pony Club and deck out both animal and rider in all the necessary gear.

From an early age children are led around on the rein by proud parents. Riding lessons are paid for. Soon the child is learning to hop her pony over a low pole on the first step towards the realisation of a dream. A showjumper in the family! An eventer! Fame! Sponsorship! Television!

Hold on a moment. Whose dream is this? What girl of eight or nine would coolly envisage a whole career in her new hobby, particularly when she has barely got started at school?

No, it is not the girl's dream. It is the parent (or perhaps both parents) who is manipulating the dream. It is a parent's ego which is being massaged, and titillated with future visions of Hickstead, Olympia, Aachen, or wherever.

Such parents make it plain they want their child to be a winner from the very first gymkhana. Equestrian events are by their nature difficult and very competitive, and the child who intends to do well has an awful lot to think about and do, what with staying on the horse, jumping the jumps, beating the clock, and so on. It is hardly surprising that some young riders start to develop a win-at-all-costs attitude, unfortunately at the expense of the horse. In most sports the buck stops with the sportsman. For riders, though, it does not have to. They can divert any blame on to the horse.

The horse now takes on a secondary role in the grim pursuit of rosettes, cups and medals. Young riders are still too immature to see what is happening. The skills they display at horse trials and other events are wonderful to see. But when things go wrong, the tears flow, the shame and misery of letting the team down sweep to the fore, swamping any pleasure at simply having taken part. Amateur kids start behaving like the worst kind of professional sportsman – and woe betide the horse.

I once saw one particular girl at an outdoor showjumping event. In front of a large audience, her horse refused at one of the fences. She brought it round again, gave it a sharp reminder with the whip and approached the fence for the second time. At the last moment, the horse refused again. Now she was angry and really whipped the horse. She no longer had any thought for the animal. In her mind – and she was no novice but an experienced horsewoman – it was *her* failure which mattered most. Never mind that the horse clearly could not cope with that particular fence – she saw herself being disgraced in public and could not handle the idea.

As she left the ring, I could see she had not got over her rage at what the horse had 'done to her'. There was something else in her mind, I could tell. I decided to follow her.

She rode out of the ring, then took the horse down behind a line of bushes. By the time I caught up with her, she had dismounted and was really leathering the horse with her whip.

I snatched the whip and gave her a piece of my mind. She stood there boiling with silent rage, and then accused me of interfering. Anyway, she maintained, she was not causing the horse any harm.

Luckily I received ready support from the judges of the event. From their offices on top of a double-decker bus they had clearly seen the whole sorry episode. They would take care of her, they promised me, and so they did. I was happy to leave the matter in their hands. A severe reprimand from the showjumping authorities would carry more weight with this girl, I thought, than a scolding from an outsider such as myself.

That girl and I would not see eye to eye for some time – not until she developed the maturity to realise that a horse and rider must be equal partners, sharing success and failure and always ready to look forward to another day. Today when I watch her ride, I see that she has acquired the attitude of a responsible horsewoman.

Much more to my taste was another rider at the same event. He had entered for the fun of it and by the time he and his horse had completed their round he had knocked up at least thirty faults. He came in, jumped off the horse, patted it and gave it a hug. 'Thanks for getting me round,' he said.

I will always remember him. A true amateur who loved his horse, he showed the spirit that day which I would offer as a model for all young riders. His horse had got him round, and that was more than enough. The faults were forgotten. They counted for nothing. What this man did was to praise his horse for all the successful jumps they had made together, the ones where they *didn't* kick the pole off. To him, that was the great achievement. I could not agree more. Jeremy, I salute you.

NEGLECT

OWNERS WHO ARE UNFIT TO CARE FOR ANIMALS

When poverty and mental ill-health go hand in hand, the effect on pet animals can be disastrous. If some of the decision-makers in the National Health Service, and their Government bosses, saw at first hand what really happens, they might be less keen to release mentally-ill patients into the community before they are properly equipped for life in the outside world.

In this book my concern is the avoidance of animal suffering, and it is a sad fact that dogs, cats and other pets need protection from these unfortunate people. It would be one of the great benefits of a pet or dog registration scheme if all prospective owners had to show in advance that they were capable of looking after an animal and had the necessary resources. It would not solve everything, but it would certainly be a start if some kind of screening process were in operation. Where mentally unstable people were concerned, this would act as an invaluable filter to deter, say, someone who lived on his own, without family support, from acquiring a pet.

There would still be abuses. A person in a disturbed state may be impervious to the laws of the land. You can fine him for ill-treating an animal; he refuses or neglects to pay the fine. You can ban him from keeping an animal, having already taken his last pet into care. What does he do? He goes out and gets another one, if necessary by stealing it from someone's garden.

Two men, I will call them Alan and Robert, both had a long history of mental illness and were treated for their condition in hospital. The time came when the authorities decided to release them into the community. Alan was given a council flat to live in, and Robert was allocated a back-to-back house in another part of the city. A friendship existed between the two men, and they kept in touch after leaving hospital.

The first to come to my notice was Alan. His flat was one of four in a block on a council estate. I went round there and he opened the door. He was dirty and unkempt, and the flat was a tip. He was obviously unable to cope on his own, despite the money he received from Social Security.

In the flat I found two dogs. One was chained to the back of a washing machine in the kitchen and was in poor condition. The other was dead. He lay in Alan's bedroom on an old sack beside the bed. When I looked more closely I saw that he had been dead for several days, and was infested with second-generation maggots. The body was decomposing and the smell in the room was indescribable.

Obviously Alan had not received any kind of support from social workers for a long time. No-one could have gone into that flat and found the conditions in any way tolerable.

Alan was taken to court, and he was banned for life from keeping a dog. The next time I saw him, it was to check up on a report that he had ignored the ban and got himself another dog. I found Alan at Robert's house. Both Robert and Alan had a dog, and both animals were in a terrible state.

So then Robert was taken to court. The magistrates gave him a conditional discharge for two years and disqualified him from keeping a dog for five years. In the meantime Alan's condition had deteriorated further and I managed to get him taken into a hostel. The dog was also taken into care.

It then emerged that Robert had been terrorising Alan. He was known to be a violent man and his neighbours were frightened of him. He preyed on others down on their luck, offering to take them into his house and then robbing them of whatever they had.

The dog that was the subject of Robert's court case – a black and tan cross-bred dog – had been stolen. Robert had found the dog tied to a drainpipe of a nearby house and had taken him. Luckily, the owner had reported the loss and we were able to reunite him and his dog.

I then found that Robert had a second dog, a tan and white cross-bred collie. His behaviour towards this dog was equally cruel. It was reported to me that he kept taking the animal out and dumping it on the other side of the city. Each time the dog found its way back home, Robert took him out again and tried to lose him. I took possession of the dog and had him examined by a vet. Unfortunately the condition of the dog was such that he failed to respond to treatment and had to be humanely destroyed.

I also had reason to believe that Robert kept another animal at his house – a cat. I returned to the house and asked him how many other animals he had. He replied, 'None.'

I didn't believe him so one day, when I knew that Robert was out, I went to the house and spoke to another man whom he had taken in. Was there a cat living in the house which belonged to Robert, I asked. 'Yes', he replied, and invited me inside.

I found the cat, a black and white male, in some distress. He had an injury to his jaw, so I took him away for a vet to have a look at him. He examined the cat and said the injury was an unusual one. He suggested the cat could have been hit by a car some three weeks before, but had received no treatment for the injury.

The saga goes on to this day. Alan has appeared in court at least five times to date for ignoring his ban on keeping a dog. Each time a dog is removed from him, he goes and steals another one. Robert's record is scarcely better, and follows a similar pattern.

It is no good fining these men; they have no money. As for the bans, what more can the magistrates do? The men are banned already, but keep on ignoring the court's instructions. It seems to be thought that imprisonment would not be a satisfactory remedy, since both Alan and Robert would learn nothing from the experience. In the meantime they remain somewhere on the fringe of the outside world, a constant menace to the local animal population.

Not all cases of this kind are quite as complex as the sorry saga of Alan and Robert, but it angers me that this type of crime is so frequent. Here is another example.

Two brothers, aged 59 and 61 years, lived together in a house on a council estate. Neither could read or write. They had already been banned from keeping dogs for failing to provide their animals with proper care and attention – an act of omission. But one of the brothers went further. He obtained another dog on which he carried out an act of commission, namely he hanged the dog from the upstairs window, in a noose, till it died.

He claimed the dog had fallen out of the window, but this was too much even for his brother who, it would appear, despite being already convicted of causing suffering, had slightly higher standards. He could not condone such a matter and in front of me told his brother so. The truth thus came out, and when taken before the courts the younger brother found himself banned for life from keeping a dog and placed under supervision.

In such extreme cases, there is only one answer. These men are not fit to live in society because they are incapable of understanding, let alone respecting, our basic laws and codes. They also have no one to look after them.

There are many such people needing supervision who are a menace to animals. There is no easy answer to this problem, but the closure of the many hospitals in which these people were cared for is in my opinion a retrograde step, both for their welfare and the welfare of animals.

Dealing with such cases is a perpetual thorn in the side of animal welfare bodies. It drives me close to despair that so many dogs and cats are sacrificed in the cause of a bad Health policy. I see so many pet owners who are glaringly incapable of taking a responsible place in our society – and yet the Government supports them. They pitch them straight out into a house or flat, and in effect wash their hands of them.

In my opinion there should be many more halfway houses where the mentally ill can have time to rehabilitate themselves under the eye of a warden and psychiatric helpers. In such a set-up it might be a good idea – an extension of the PAT-Dog Scheme (see For Those Who Serve at the back of this book) – to introduce a pet into the home which the inmates could learn to share and look after. When they finally rejoined the community on a full-time basis, many would surely be much better equipped to cope with the disciplines of owning a pet – shopping for food, serving the food, grooming, exercising and so on. Their training would help them to become better and more fulfilled as owners. They could rightly take personal pride in what they had done, the animal would be healthier and more responsive, and the relationship between the two could then grow firmer and deeper.

THOSE WITH THE WRONG PRIORITIES

How many people would willingly starve their dog or cat? Very few, I like to think. But sometimes I wonder.

In nearly every case I came across, unless the offender was mentally ill, the animal has been starved because its owner's social priorities were woefully out of order.

There is a pattern to these cases. I used to find that usually the owner was out of work and had no money to feed the dog. Or so he would say. But if I looked round the room I stood in, I would see a big television set and a video. There would be a packet of cigarettes on the table. He and his wife lived rent-free, on Social Security. I would find out that she went to bingo; he liked his pint. There would be hardly any food in the house but they, the humans, were not starving.

Why then, I would ask again, could he not feed the dog properly? No money, he would say, and the story began all over again. It always shocked me that people could have this attitude. When I visited homes fitted with modern machines and various creature comforts, but with no food for the dog, I was appalled. I still am. It is not *necessary* for any domestic animal to suffer in this way.

These people have got to get their priorities sorted out. People seem to demand so much more for themselves, and they want it now, as of right. That includes entertainment. They may fully accept that they are badly off, and that there is much they cannot afford. But this, by some extraordinary twist of logic, is seen as an added reason for going to bingo and squandering £5.

'If I didn't go out, I'd go mad sitting here,' they would say to me. This might be so. But £5 also buys 12 tins of dog food.

One couple I visited had a history of social problems. Of their three children, one was in local authority care, one was in the care of a relative, and the other one fended for himself. Also in the house were two cats and two dogs. They were in a terrible state. The younger cat weighed 2lb, the older one 3^1/$_2$lb. The stomachs of both were tucked, their bones jutted like bent sticks against their coats. When offered food, they ate ravenously, as though they had not seen food for days.

The first dog – a black, tan and white female – had recently had puppies but there was no milk in her teats. She was extremely thin, and weighed 15lb instead of the 35lb she should have weighed. When offered food, she wolfed it down – and then started gnawing at the dish. The second dog was in no better condition. Both required hospital treatment.

The wife, who was the real owner, signed all the animals over to the RSPCA with evident relief. When I talked to them separately it was clear that the husband took no responsibility for the animals. They were the wife's, he said, it was up to her to feed them.

'You knew they were hungry, didn't you?' I asked him.

'Yes,' he replied.

'But you didn't seek any help for them.'

'I didn't know I could.'

He went on to say that he was hardly ever at home, and admitted that the animals were left to fend for themselves. It then emerged that he and his wife obtained food for their own consumption through the Social Services.

I said to him, 'So you told your social worker when you had no food?'

'Yes,' he said.

'You could have told your social worker you had no food for your animals,' I went on.

He did not reply.

'You agree that they were starving,' I said.

'Yes,' he said.

To the wife I said, 'All your animals, the two dogs and the two cats, were in poor condition. Did you ever take them to a vet?'

'No.'

'Why not?'

'There was nowt wrong with them.'

Like her husband, she often went off and left the animals.

'Who is responsible for feeding them when you are away?' I asked her.

'I can't feed them unless I have money,' was her answer.

'So the dogs and cats have at times been left without food for days.'

'Yes, that's right.'

'Whose responsibility is it for feeding the animals?'

'Mine.'

There was no option but to take them to court. Although they had given up control of their present animals, there was good reason, born of experience, to think they might well collect other animals in the future, thus repeating the whole miserable cycle. They were found guilty of causing unnecessary suffering to all four animals, fined and banned for life from keeping a dog.

It was the best we could do. By bringing the action, we had secured legal protection for animals who might otherwise have become future sufferers at the neglectful hands of this couple.

What angers me in such cases is that the owners cared so little for their animals. A call for help to their social worker would have saved so much suffering. The animals could have gone into care, giving the couple time to sort out whether they really wanted, or could afford to give a good home, with regular feeding, to two dogs and two cats. It would have made them take a hard look at themselves, and at how they wanted to spend the little money they had.

At rock-bottom rates, the weekly cost today of feeding all four must be at least £10, with no allowance for vet's fees. And that means £10 every week, without fail, for the rest of the animals' lives.

This couple had had every opportunity to act and save the animals. Whether through pride, despair, or a mixture of both, they did nothing.

At the back of their minds there might also have been another, unspoken fear of robbery and the resultant feeling that they needed a dog to guard the house. This is becoming more and more widespread, and not just in the inner-city areas. People may not have much worth stealing, but a video is portable and easily removed, and so is the cash from gas and electricity meters. They know that thieves are about in their neighbourhood, so they get a dog. They tie it to a post at the bottom of the garden or leave it loose indoors when they go out during the day.

These dogs are left alone for hours on end, often without food and water – and, worst of all, without companionship. Isolation such as this runs completely against their nature. Dogs are pack animals and need company. Without it, they are bored out of their minds. To leave any dog alone in a house or flat for eight to ten hours a day is cruel. Unfortunately, such cruelty is common. Take this case:

A 59-year-old man, living alone in a flat on a council estate, took dogs off the street and confined them in his flat. They seldom saw daylight, and dogs and bitches soon began breeding.

On my first visit to the flat, to which the council had tried to gain entry for fumigation purposes, I found the dogs suffering from very bad skin conditions (which the vet later confirmed as being sarcoptic mange). There was urine soaking the carpets and a foul smell came from a cupboard in the corner of the hallway. In it I found a number of dead puppies – these were the case of the stench.

All offers of help were refused by the tenant and as a result, court proceedings had to be instituted. The Stipendary Magistrate placed the man on probation for three years and ordered that he should confine himself to keeping just one dog. A very sensible decision under the circumstances.

A dog has so much to give including affection and loyalty, and that special quality of dogginess which it alone possesses. To deny any dog the opportunity to use its abilities, and show off its qualities, is cruel and thoughtless – one more instance of human selfishness riding roughshod over the needs of animals.

Acts of neglect towards animals are not confined to dogs, or to cats, horses and ponies. Even polecats are sometimes subjected to such treatment. A young accounts clerk appeared before magistrates and was convicted of causing unnecessary suffering to his polecat. This 19-year-old lived in a bed-sit and struck up a friendship with a lad who lived some two miles away. He bought a polecat and asked if he could leave it overnight in the garage at his young friend's home. The boy's mother agreed to it, but just for the one night.

Despite many warnings and requests the polecat was not moved and the young man ceased to visit it. The young boy and his family were frightened to go near the animal, and finally the polecat died of starvation.

In court the chairman of the bench told the young man, 'This is an extremely serious matter. When you accept the responsibility for an animal the court expects you to look after and care for it.' If only more people could hear that message. But they don't. People are thoughtless, and sometimes it seems never to occur to them that in doing whatever they feel like doing, they cause needless misery.

When faced with the reality of what suffering they caused to an animal, it is amazing what people will say to justify their actions.

Take the case of a 21-year-old unemployed man who decided to move in with his girlfriend, who lived some seven or eight miles away from the flat he had been allocated by the local council.

He simply upped and left one day, shutting the door behind him. In doing do, he locked his dog inside the empty flat. His mother had a key but had no idea that he had left a dog in the flat, and she had no reason now to go and visit. The result was that the dog starved to death. I found this poor animal lying on a plastic bag. It was obvious that the dog had even been trying to eat plastic in its desperation. In his post mortem, the vet revealed that the stomach contained just three pieces of polythene similar to the material used in the manufacture of plastic bags.

When questioned, the young man stated that he moved because he felt ill and was only going to live for another year. He claimed he had a growth on his kidney that was nearly touching his heart. He is still going strong today. This medical claim was not put forward in court, where he was fined £200 and ordered to pay £128.75p in costs. He was also disqualified from keeping any animal for 15 years.

THOSE WHO BUY ON IMPULSE

This problem affects every kind of pet, but to illustrate it I want to focus on horses and ponies. They are seductive beasts. They win the hearts of young, and not-so-young, girls and boys who are hooked, and want to own one for themselves.

In the past, ownership was largely confined to wealthy suburbanites and farming people with all the space they needed to keep the animal properly. Not any longer. Today, ponies are relatively cheap to buy; not necessarily the best ponies, but over-breeding seems to count for little. There is a big market for horses and ponies, and breeders and dealers eagerly combine to supply it.

A deal is struck, the purchase made. Only now, in far too many cases that I have come across, does the new owner give serious thought to where to put the pony. If they have no land of their own, and cannot afford to rent a field or paddock, they tether it out anywhere they can, on council ground or whatever else is available.

At first, all goes well. The girl or boy sees the pony at least twice a day, and takes food and water down to it. Then the other demands of life impose themselves once more. There is school to go to, homework to be done. They skip going down in the morning and look after the pony just once a day. Time goes by, and the novelty wears off more or less completely. Soon the pony is being left to look after itself.

It can't, of course. The land around its tether quickly becomes horse-tired, or barren, and the pony, without supplementary feeding, grows ill. There is no money for vet's fees, and sooner or later an animal charity has to intervene.

An awful lot of suffering could be avoided if only people would think more carefully before they buy. As with all animals, the initial cost of buying a pony is nothing compared with the continuing cost of its daily upkeep, not all of which is payable in money. The pony needs food, certainly, and veterinary care when necessary. If it is to be ridden, there is also the cost of the tack, or stable gear. Then there is the human contribution – the time an owner must give to grooming, exercising and providing companionship for the animal. Although a horse is more independent than, say, a dog, it still thrives on company and a close relationship with its owner; when this is withdrawn, the horse suffers.

If a horse is to be kept out, whether on the owner's land or somewhere else, a lot of consideration should go into the suitability of that piece of land.

Does it offer any shelter for the horse? Shelter is all-important. No horse should be left tethered out if it has no means of getting away from a cold prevailing wind, and avoiding the added chill factor which brings the temperature down even further if the animal is virtually static. Ideally, the horse should have a three-sided shelter which it can walk into; the back of the shelter should face the prevailing wind. A wall in a similar position is better than nothing. The important thing to remember is that the wind is the chief enemy, far more so than rain.

People have said to me, 'But wild horses don't mind the weather. Those ponies in the New Forest or on Dartmoor, they live out all the time and it doesn't do them any harm.'

'Well', I would answer, ' it would do if they didn't have the freedom to go and look for shelter.'

That is the big difference. Wild ponies are not tethered. If they wish, they can run for miles to find conditions which suit them. It is nonsense to claim that wild animals can do without shelter. They need protection from chilling winds just as much as other animals. If you look around, on a cold day in the country, you will see cattle bunching in the corner of a field where hedges and trees offer the thickest wind-break; or sheep taking cover in a hollow in the hillside. All these animals need some degree of shelter.

In hot weather, the sun is the enemy. Then the horse needs shade, either in the form of the three-sided (and roofed) shelter mentioned above, or else it must have some other place it can go – under a tree or beneath a wall.

In all weathers, the horse must have a regular supply of drinking water. If hot sun evaporates the water, or in cold weather the surface ices over and no-one comes to break it up, the horse is deprived of this vital supply. Remember, this horse is tethered and cannot go off and look for a stream, as the Dartmoor ponies can.

All these provisions – shelter from wind and sun, and regular drinking water – are essential for the horse's well-being. A shelter is not some kind of optional extra which the owner can put in 'for next winter, when I've got a bit of money saved up.' The horse may be dead by then.

OWNERS IN HOSPITAL

This is perhaps not so much a kind of neglect (though in extremis, neglect is the result) as an example of how local authorities and social workers sometimes fail to make services known to those in need. As a result, both owner and animal can suffer. I get letters all the time from people, many of them elderly, who need to go into hospital for an operation. Then they put it off, and put it off again, because they are so frightened of what will happen to their dog or cat when they are away. They cannot afford boarding fees, they tell me – and at £5 a day that is no joke for a single pensioner without private means. They feel trapped, and would rather sacrifice themselves by not having the operation than risk losing their pet.

An old lady wrote to me saying that she badly needed an operation, but she had an old dog and a budgie. She was worried stiff that if she went into hospital she would never see them again.

I went round to her house. 'It will be all right,' I explained to her. 'You have a legal right to have your pets looked after by the local authority. You go and have your operation, and your dog will be well looked after while you are in hospital. *And* the budgie,' I added quickly, as soon as I saw a distressed look cross her face.

For a long time she would not believe me. It was quite obvious that she had never heard of this right until then. And yet it is no secret. So why had no-one told her? Surely, among all the social workers, doctors and nurses she had seen, someone must have known about it and could have put her fears to rest.

The law is quite clear. Under the National Assistance Act 1948 (Section 48), if someone has to go into hospital, and has no relative or friend who can look after their pets, then it is up to the local authority to take charge of them until the person is released from hospital. The actual wording refers to taking charge of all 'goods and chattels,' which most definitely includes animals.

The local authority has a duty to place the pets in care, and the responsibility for paying the boarding fees at the kennels or animal home also rests with them. If only this law were more widely known, think how many pet owners would be saved all that anxiety.

These days, councils are very budget-conscious and you will not find this service advertised. It does exist, however, and people should feel free to make use of it. When the hospital treatment is over, and the person goes home and is reunited with his pets, the local authority has the right to ask the pet owner to make a contribution towards its costs. This is a matter for negotiation, and those who plainly cannot pay must stand up for their rights and say so. If necessary, they can call on their local Citizens' Advice Bureau to help them.

Let there be no doubt about this. The funds are there for the local authority to use. There is an Act of Parliament which says so.

I also want to emphasise that the duty rests with the local authority alone. It is not up to the RSPCA, the Cat's Protection League, the Canine Defence League or any other animal charity to provide accommodation for pets in these circumstances. It is up to your local council to do it.

In my own area, Leeds City Council have been very fair in this respect. They sometimes need chasing and reminding, but they are a good deal better than some local authorities whose only thought is to try and foist the responsibility for these cases onto one of the animal charities.

TAKING BIRDS FROM THE WILD

It was always part of my work as an RSPCA Inspector to deal with cases where people were unlawfully taking protected birds. The type of offender varied widely, from the private collector to someone who knew he can sell a bird on for profit. There are taxidermists who buy birds taken in this way, and there is a lucrative racket in protected species such as hawks and other birds of prey. Motorway service stations are a common venue for handing over birds and collecting the cash.

Wild birds: the legal position

The laws concerning wild birds are immensely complicated. I wish they were a lot easier to grasp. If they were, I am sure some offences would not be committed.

One of the main reasons why there are so many different legal Schedules of Birds is that there have to be separate categories to distinguish between game birds, pest species, birds which may sold alive, others which may be sold dead, and so on. To understand the whole story, you need to have a specialised knowledge of the intricacies of relevant legislation. I recommend anyone who wants to find out all the details, not just of the Schedules but of the exceptions to them and other bits of fine print, to contact the Royal Society for the Protection of Birds.

They produce an excellent booklet called *Wild Birds and The Law*, summarising the provisions in the Wildlife and Countryside Act 1981 which relate to bird protection. In general, as the booklet explains, the basic principle of the Act is that 'all wild birds, their nests and eggs are protected by law and some rare species are afforded special protection'. For everyday purposes, that is all the average reader needs to know. It would certainly be no bad thing if young people were brought up to believe that all wild birds should be respected and left alone, together with their nests and eggs, at all times of the year. Full stop.

The punishments are severe. Fines range up to £400 for most offences and up to £2,000 for killing or taking a Schedule 1 bird (those protected by special penalties at all times). Moreover, each offence against a bird, nest, egg or skin is treated separately, so if someone steals six eggs they are liable to receive six fines.

Too tame to return to the wild

Many birds are taken with the idea of keeping them and turning them into a pet. This is completely wrong. Firstly, a wild bird has the right to remain wild and no-one should interfere with its day-to-day existence in nature. Secondly, the longer a bird is kept indoors, away from its natural habitat, the harder it becomes for the bird to survive in the wild when it is released. It may become tame, and it always becomes dependent on its keeper to provide it with food. In both these situations it loses the ability to fend for itself and acquires other unsuitable habits which are unnatural to it. The keeper 'imprints' the bird with an alien way of life. No-one has the right to do this.

Birds *can* be released successfully into the wild, but it is a difficult and complicated process which only a qualified expert should undertake. I cannot emphasise this too strongly because for many people, particularly young offenders, it is the last thing they think of. For them the principal allure of taking birds lies in the hunt and the capture. After that, they soon lose interest, and the bird is left to suffer. It suffers whether it remains in captivity until it dies, or is put back in the wild where it is unable to cope and dies anyway.

I have known a number of cases involving jays and jackdaws. The bird is found injured in some way and then someone takes it in to look after it. The bird recovers, but the host keeps it too long and it grows tame. Eventually the bird, having retained enough of its old instincts, becomes too much for its hosts – messing up the house or making too much noise – and they return it to the wild.

The bird, however, is reluctant to leave its new area. Then reports appear in the newspaper of a mad bird which is attacking babies in prams or divebombing housewives in the street.

It's the same bird, the rescued jay or jackdaw. All it is doing is trying to be friendly. It got used to flying around and landing on someone's shoulder when it lived in a house, and now it is repeating the act. People see it as mad and dangerous, but in fact it is only acting strangely – unlike a 'real' wild bird – because it has lost its fear of humans.

It was a human, of course, who caused the trouble in the first place. It always is.

MANKIND'S GREED

Mass production is seen in many industries as a quick way to profit, but where animals are concerned, this can lead to a life of misery and suffering.

Take the battery hen for instance: she is sentenced to a life of imprisonment in a pen she shares with others, and all the law requires is that she be given a space, equivalent to a foolscap sheet of paper, to live in. She has no privacy while she lays her eggs. What mother would put up with that? But while the housewife demands cheap eggs, instead of paying just that little extra for free-range eggs, then there will always be those willing to supply them.

To take another example, calves spend their short lives confined in a crate to provide the pale meat thought of as a delicacy by some. Is this worth it?

Calves are not alone in their predicament: pigs and even rabbits are intensely reared for their meat. In the case of rabbits they are also farmed for their fur. All this is to help man obtain just that little bit more out of life.

Some of the worst examples of greed-inspired cruelty involve those unfortunate bitches who provide owners of puppy farms with a living and here I want to discuss this activity in greater detail.

THE PUPPY FARMERS

Every so often, the media focus on the puppy-farming racket. They usually call it a 'new' animal scandal, as if they have uncovered it for the first time, but to me both the story and the images are depressingly familiar: the battered sheds and damp pens hardly bigger than rabbit hutches; the worn-out, sad-eyed breeding bitches; the dealer stacking boxes full of puppies in his van ready for the stifling drive from Wales to some distant kennels; the stink and neglect everywhere, so strong that you can feel it just from looking at the pictures.

I welcome the efforts of the newspaper and television journalists. Anything that can move public opinion against the sordid practices of the puppy farmers is a step in the right direction. However, real progress has been painfully slow since I first witnessed the filthy, prison-like conditions of many of the breeding farms in Wales, more than seventeen years ago.

In 1978 I completed a report on the *Breeding, Selling and Transit of Puppies and Dogs in Mid-Wales, 1974-1977* and presented it to the Headquarters of the RSPCA. I then moved from my posting in Wales to the North East of England, which took me away from the hill farms that are at the centre of the puppy racket in Britain.

Today it distresses me to find that some of the same breeders and dealers, who were my opponents then, are still in business, and that by all accounts new breeders have entered the area, encouraged by the lax attitude of the local authorities.

Others to enter the trade were farmers hit by Common Market restrictions on dairy produce. Some were even encouraged to take up dog breeding by the Government's Agricultural Development and Advisory Service (ADAS), to make up their lost income. When challenged about this, an ADAS spokesman replied, 'We are no longer advocating it, but at the same time it should not be ruled out completely.'

The statement has that special ring of ignorance about it which plagued my own time in Wales. So many people in authority had no idea what was going on, or did not want to know. It took me more than a year of pleading and persuasion to arouse their interest and secure some degree of support.

The law was not fundamentally at fault. It was simply that, to my amazement, people were reluctant to enforce it. The hills were riddled with dog breeders breaking numerous provisions covered by the Pet Animals Act 1951, the Animal Boarding Establishments Act 1963, the Breeding of Dogs Act 1973, and later by the Transport of Animals (Road and Rail) Order 1975.

I would investigate a complaint, then if it was justified I turned to the local authority for help, only to meet a wall of silence. If I complained more loudly, I was accused of seeking publicity. Outrageous denials were issued to excuse this inertia. At least, I thought it was inertia until I found there might be other motives.

Several local officials were involved in puppy farming themselves. They were part of a cosy network of breeders and dealers who traded amongst themselves. One might be a breeder, another might buy puppies off that breeder and distribute them to pet shops in England.

What distressed me most about these people, and those they covered for, was the cruel nature of the trade they condoned. For me, animals come first. Yet here was a rampant puppy trade which depended on the merciless exploitation of breeding bitches to supply a market dominated by commercial considerations.

The bitches were condemned to a lifetime of squalor and abuse, imprisoned in bleak quarters on some windswept farm or smallholding. When they had outlived their usefulness, many were dumped – thrown into slurry pits, drowned in water butts or crudely banged on the head.

I wanted to stop these abuses, and to shut down the primitive, unhygienic farms on which they took place. It was to prove a long uphill struggle. Breeding and dealing were, and are, lucrative trades for those who practise them with the necessary ruthless efficiency. They will always appeal as occupations to people prepared to ignore the needs of animals in order to profit from them.

These breeders can only be fought within the law; and the laws which affect the puppy farmers are clearly not tight enough to restrain illicit traders in dogs and puppies.

Take the breeders, for example. Anyone who keeps more than two breeding bitches and wishes to trade commercially is legally obliged to apply for a breeder's licence under the Breeding of Dogs Act 1973. When I first went to work in Wales as an RSPCA Inspector, this was a relatively new Act, deeply unpopular with some of the locals. They did not want their premises to be inspected, knowing that they were sub-standard. Some even complained that the Act imposed unfairly high standards and did not allow for country dwellers living at subsistence level.

It was a corrupt view, but it took hold in many minds, encouraging a spirit of rebellion. These breeders looked around for loopholes. If they did not apply for a breeder's licence, how could they get away with it?

One way was to claim that the breeding bitch was exempt from the new law because it was kept as a pet. As they well knew, it is not illegal to sell puppies which have been produced by a family pet. Many opted for this route, selling their puppies on to middle-men or through carefully worded advertisements in the local newspaper. These made no mention of breeding kennels, and always purported to be from private individuals who had a few surplus puppies for sale.

Remaining on the unlicensed side of the business had another important attraction. Once a licence had been applied for and granted, the local council's representatives had the right to enter such premises at all reasonable times without giving prior warning, but they had no right of access to the farms and smallholdings of unlicensed breeders. Such breeders could refuse admission, which made it well-nigh impossible to amass the evidence necessary for a successful prosecution under the Act.

Breeders also relied on the remoteness of their farms to keep them safe from probing eyes. From the back roads between Aberystwyth and Lampeter, stony tracks unmarked on any map twist uninvitingly into an anonymous countryside. Further east, in the shadow of the Cambrian Mountains, it was even easier to become invisible in that bleak and undulating landscape. It would take a serious investigator months to visit every shack and tumbledown cottage in the area – and well those illicit breeders knew it. They kept their heads down, and declined to be counted.

In 1979 there were 76 breeders licensed by one authority. I estimated that at least 200 more were breeding dogs without a licence. Similar figures were produced for a neighbouring authority, where the District Council licensed about 120 breeders a year and the RSPCA Inspector put the figure for unlicensed farms at around 300. Today there are still unlicensed breeders operating in these areas.

There is a good example of close links between breeders and the local authorities. The owner of a stud dog establishment was also a member of the Environmental Health, Licensing and Public Works Committee of a local authority.

I first went to see him after a woman in Ripon, North Yorkshire complained that she had been sold a sick corgi puppy. Her sister had collected him from a pet shop in Bradford without carefully inspecting the animal. The new owner in Ripon was appalled by the puppy's condition and took him to a local vet, who examined the puppy, said to be nine weeks old, and reported:

'This pup was showing clinical signs of conjunctivitis, tonsillitis, rhinitis and pneumonia which in my opinion is indicative of a case of canine distemper. Apart from this, the pup had clinical signs of rickets, and mange of the ear funnel, legs and ventral abdomen.'

The corgi was clearly sick and should not have been offered for sale. When the Bradford RSPCA Inspector looked into the matter he found that the puppy had been delivered by rail three days before he was sold.

It emerged that the local official was deeply involved with the puppy trade. He ran a stud farm, to which other breeders brought their bitches to be mated with his dogs. He would then arrange to buy the litters back and sold them on through his many outlets in England. It was common for his puppies to be transported over long distances by rail. In his part of the country he was one of British Rail's biggest account holders for the transport of puppies.

Another complaint against him came in around that time. He had sent a consignment of tea chests containing five corgis and two poodles to a dealer in Great Yarmouth. The 350-mile journey to Yarmouth, involving a cross-London trip between Paddington and Liverpool Street, lasted 14 hours. It was August and conditions were particularly hot and humid, but the animals were not fed and watered during the journey. The tea chests were opened at Yarmouth; the poodles though distressed were still alive, but three of the five corgi pups were dead.

British Rail did not contact the local RSPCA Inspector about the incident; he heard about it several hours later from a newspaper reporter. Anxious to examine the puppies, he traced them next day to a Yarmouth pet shop but found that the owner had already buried the dead puppies. The Inspector obtained an exhumation order, dug them up and arranged for a vet to carry out a post-mortem. Too late; the bodies had already begun to decompose and the vet was unable to ascertain the precise cause of death. He thought they had died from heat exhaustion.

It was impossible, therefore, to obtain any picture of how fit the puppies were before they began their journey. British Rail was singularly unhelpful too, claiming that it had been an 'excellent transit, particularly as cross-London transport was involved.' The BR spokesman added:

'There was no need to doubt that the livestock was fit to travel, and it was certainly well packed.'

How British Rail could have known either of these things was never made clear. The tea chest was not available for inspection; it had been broken up.

I was asked by RSPCA Headquarters to call on the sender, to inspect his stock and examine the packing cases he used to dispatch animals from his establishment.

To my astonishment, I found that he did not have a licence to deal in animals. When I challenged him on this, he said, 'I had better get one.'

Even after my visit he did not take out a licence. I chased him for months about this, and eventually brought in the local press and television to help my cause. At last under this pressure he obtained the appropiate licence.

In the wake of the Yarmouth affair, when the three corgis died, I came to a new arrangement with British Rail. Impressed by my argument that they would be held responsible if they accepted crates that were unsuitable, they agreed to call me when such crates arrived at departure stations. They sharpened their scrutiny of livestock in transit, and began refusing to accept consignments which fell below the requirements of the Transport of Animals (Road and Rail) Order 1975.

I took successful action against several other breeders and dealers. A common thread in these cases was their appalling disregard for hygiene and cleanliness. One is given at length in the Casebook section of this book. These are others:

- An unlicensed breeder of poodles moved to Wales after trouble with the authorities over breeding dogs elsewhere. She lived in unbelievable conditions in a bungalow with about thirty dogs. Excrement lay on the floor in every room. The smell was appalling. She responded by saying she could live like a pig if she wanted. The vet testified that she caused unnecessary suffering to the dogs by forcing them to inhale ammonia from their own urine. She was fined and left the area.

- Another breeder sold dogs without a licence in a back room of a pub. The floor was covered in filth, and puppies were kept there in a cardboard box. All her dogs and puppies were in poor health. In the very next room she cooked food for her customers. She was convicted of cruelty and banned from keeping dogs for 12 months.

- A third case involved a dealer who bred sheepdogs and housed them in the back of a small van near the house leaving the bitches to whelp in a cardboard box in all weathers. One dog was found dead on his premises. The local authority took him to court for causing a health hazard but he started breeding again and was later prosecuted for causing unnecessary suffering to a dog.

FARMING PROBLEMS

Farming is hard. No-one would dispute that. The hours are terrible, the conditions are physically rigorous, no matter how many machines a farmer may buy in to help him. Markets are volatile and the dictates of politicians in both London and Brussels are a perpetual source of harassment. Sometimes would-be farmers, especially those leaving the city or town for a country life, fail to realise just how demanding a farm and its animals can be.

One such person who changed direction was a man who gave up his town life and bought a smallholding. He bought cattle and sheep to stock his farm, but had no knowledge of livestock, nor did he seek assistance or take help when it was offered. Soon his cattle began to die, and despite further offers of help, he still refused it. In the end he appeared in court, where he was fined for omitting to provide 20 cows with necessary care and attention. This caused him to see sense and realise there was more to farming than just buying in the cattle.

All in all, I think the British farmer does as well as he can. He has to be highly efficient, or he will go under. If at times he is over-thrifty, he nevertheless looks after his animals to a standard which must be amongst the highest in the world. There are times, however, when things go drastically wrong. When they do, the animals are the first to suffer.

During my years in Wales, a militant sheep farmer took it into his head to start blowing up pipes supplying water from Wales to England. He was caught and taken into custody.

It then came to light that there was no-one else to look after his farm. The RSPCA was forced to intervene. My colleague on the next station had to take on – in addition to his other duties – the exhausting job of looking after this man's sheep. The work included seeing the flock through a lambing season, and was a physically draining experience that did him no good at all.

This is another case where we should have a Government Inspectorate staffed with trained officers who could take over the running of a farm when a real emergency arises.

The law already provides for this. In 1964 a special committee was appointed by the Government to look into the welfare of animals on farms, in particular those which were raised by intensive methods. Its recommendations led to the passing of the Agriculture (Miscellaneous Provisions) Act of 1968. The Act made it an offence to 'cause or permit unnecessary pain or distress' to livestock on agricultural land.

The provisions of the Act are wide and cover, for example, failure to maintain the cages in a poultry unit, or failure to milk a cow. In a case involving the former, the magistrates found that the hens had been caused unnecessary distress, while the cow, in another case, had been caused unnecessary pain when the farmer refused to milk the herd.

Section 6 of the Act authorises the Minister of Agriculture to instruct members of the State Veterinary Service – usually known as Ministry Vets – 'to enter, at any reasonable time, with such other persons who are considered necessary on to any land, except premises used wholly or mainly as a dwelling [in other words, a farmhouse], for the purpose of examining livestock'.

The wording leaves no doubt in my mind that it is the responsibility of Ministry Vets to examine livestock that may be suffering, and also to ensure that it is properly cared for in the longer term. In practice, this does not happen. Ministry Vets seem notoriously unwilling to find fault with farmers. It does not help that their area of jurisdiction covers both Agriculture and Food. This can sometimes cloud an issue, as with a farmer who is a good grain producer but too casual with his animals. In such a case, the Ministry Vet may choose to look the other way, allowing the farmer's positive record to outweigh his deficiencies.

To me this is a significant flaw in the system, and needs to be looked at. There are others too. The Ministry Vets claim that their department is always understaffed. It might be, but I sense an underlying reluctance to carry out responsibilities which is more disturbing. It comes down to this: if the Ministry Vets are not prepared to see that justice is done, and that farm animals are adequately housed and cared for, then who is?

They, after all, are the officers of a Government ministry and they alone have certain powers, including the automatic right of access to farm property. A voluntary body, such as the RSPCA, does not share this right. In my years as an Inspector, I always had to work within the more restrictive provisions of the Protection of Animals Act 1911. This confers no such right of entry, nor does it contain any provision for the issue of search warrants to the officers of charitable welfare organisations.

Here, as in so many areas of animal welfare, laws exist that are not enforced. The public, I am sure, would be much happier to know that regular random inspections were being carried out by Ministry officials and that neglectful farmers were being found out and taken to court. Instead, nine times out of ten, visits to farms are cosy, pre-arranged affairs. If a farmer has been failing to bury dead animals, he gets a 'phone call from the Ministry Vet asking for an appointment to come and see him. This gives the farmer all the time he needs to clear up the mess before the official gets there. The risk of infection or disease may still be present in the ground when the vet does arrive, but if the visible signs of it have been removed, he is much less likely to detect that something is amiss.

ANIMALS IN TRANSIT
The dangers which beset farm animals do not begin and end on the farm itself. When animals are taken to market or the slaughterhouse, many have to endure horrific treatment before their brief lives are ended.

In August 1990, a British lorry carrying 439 sheep was set on fire in the French town of Thouars, about twenty miles south of the River Loire at Saumur. The lorry was parked outside an abattoir, to which the sheep had been brought for slaughter. Some sheep were roasted alive and many others received such terrible injuries that they had to be destroyed.

A month earlier, French farmers in the same region poisoned 94 sheep brought there by lorry from Britain. The farmers were protesting against what they called cheap imports of British lamb. It was putting them out of business, they claimed.

These were just two extreme examples of man's savagery towards innocent farm animals. Sheep and cattle are continually the victims of atrocious handling on long and unnecessary journeys by truck between Britain and destinations in Continental Europe.

When people in Britain saw television reports of these killings, there was a general outcry. Animal welfare groups pressed the Minister for Agriculture to ban the export of live animals for food. The RSPCA applied to the Court of Appeal and was granted a 'judicial review' to consider banning the export of live sheep from Britain. Little came of this, however, beyond proving that the Society had the right to appeal against the provisions of laws it felt were inadequate.

The affair was a reminder that farm animals are constantly caused unnecessary suffering because of human greed. Although it cannot be denied that the French farmers were responsible for that series of atrocities against the sheep, we should not forget who was responsible for sending them to France in the first place, and why they did so.

We in Britain are quick to defend our self-appointed position as a nation of animal lovers, and we are always ready to condemn other countries for their treatment of animals. Yet those who deal in animals in this country are just as guilty of thoughtless profit-seeking as those Frenchmen who sought to protect their share of the market.

It is both a national and an international problem. Here in Britain, and on the highways of Europe, you can see cattle wagons trundling along, day and night, conveying their loads of anxious and distressed animals to distant destinations where they are slaughtered. Meanwhile, other cattle wagons are travelling in the opposite direction. In other words each pair of wagons that pass is making two long and unnecessary journeys. If Wagon A delivered to Wagon B's destination, and Wagon B delivered to Wagon A's destination, a great deal of time and money would be saved. More important still, the animals in both wagons would be spared much unnecessary distress and suffering.

It should not be beyond human ingenuity for a nation such as ours to devise a regional system for the slaughter of sheep and cattle. Animals sold at a particular market would have to be slaughtered at an abattoir in the same region. The meat would then be forwarded to its final destination in carcase form by refrigerated truck.

As for animals sold to other countries for meat, they too should be killed at the nearest point of slaughter and exported as carcases. Try as I might, I cannot find any reason whatsoever for causing animals to suffer an arduous journey only to be killed on arrival.

The transportation of animals takes many forms. Although most people think initially of road transport as the principal means, we have also to consider the journeys made by animals in ships, trains and aircraft.

Transit by sea

Many animals suffer badly from what is known as Transit or Shipping Fever, and arrive at their destination very sick or even dead. Try to imagine what goes through the mind of an animal which, accustomed to having four legs planted firmly on the ground, suddenly finds itself being tossed up and down, or suddenly thrown to its feet, in the hold of a ship.

I think I can begin to tell you how it feels. My own first encounter with animals being transported abroad took place on a ship. It was an experience I shall never forget.

While based in Wales, I received a telephone call from RSPCA Headquarters in Horsham instructing me to contact the Transport Police in Fishguard. Although that was not in my area, no-one living closer was available. It seemed there was a vessel in trouble somewhere which had a consignment of cattle aboard.

I drove from Aberystwyth to Fishguard and made contact with Sergeant Walters of the Transport Police. Could he show me the vessel, I asked. He smiled. 'Follow me,' he said.

He took me over to the Harbourmaster's office. On the wall was a chart. He pointed to an area on the chart and said, 'She's about there'.

His finger indicated a spot some six miles out to sea from Strumble Head. He smiled encouragingly at me and asked, 'How are your sea-legs?' Only then did it truly dawn on me that I would have to go out and join a ship on the high seas. I looked out of the window. Even inside the harbour the waves were swollen and turbulent, crashing ashore in clouds of spume.

While Sergeant Walters arranged for a pilot boat, I was joined by Inspector Norman, the local RSPCA Inspector, who was now free to help on the case. We went on board the pilot vessel and soon were heading out to sea. On the journey out to the ship we could see smoke still rising from her as the result of a fire.

We came alongside and at this short range I could see a number of signs of fire damage. The most immediate was to the rope ladder which dangled over the side in our direction. Now considerably shorter than it had been before the fire, its blackened end swung from a tantalising distance.

Although I was wearing a life jacket, it did nothing for my confidence to be told that I was to be first to go aboard. I crouched on the side of the pilot boat and waited for the ladder to come somewhere within reach. Each time I made to grab for it a wave lifted it up and swept it beyond me. After several failures I steeled myself to take a real lunge at it. Suddenly I felt two strong pairs of Transport Police arms seize hold of me, and then I was being propelled through the air towards the ladder. I clung at it, and it held me.

Thanks to the determination of those two Transport Police officers, all those who were going aboard made the hair-raising jump without any mishap. On the deck of the cargo ship we gathered ourselves and then went to discuss the matter with the Master.

At first he denied that he spoke any English, but when I suggested to a Customs officer that we went to look at the ship's log the Captain said, in a very adequate accent, 'I will come with you.'

We learned from the Captain that the ship, registered in Panama and owned by a firm based in Lugano, Switzerland, was nine days out of Ireland, bound for Libya. For some days before fire broke out below-decks, she had been circling in the coastal waters off Fishguard. No reasons for this were offered.

Later, it also struck me as particularly odd that on the cargo papers the animals were described as being for breeding purposes; most of the cattle I saw on that ship were steers, young castrated males. I would like to meet the person who thought he was going to breed from that lot.

With Inspector Norman I went down to the holds where the unfortunate animals were penned up for their journey. What I saw was an object lesson in how *not* to convey animals by sea. I made the following notes:

• There was no fresh drinking water available.

- The cattle had fodder to eat, but a Royal Navy officer told me it was only provided after he had ordered the crew to supply it.
- The cattle were overcrowded, and unable to lie down in their pens without being stood on.
- In the lower holds the cattle were not adequately penned, and liable to injure themselves on protrusions. We had to pen them in, and did so.
- Many of the rails on the pens were insecure. Pins to hold them were missing and some of the rails had fallen inside the pens, presenting a danger of injury to the animals.
- In the lower holds the lack of ventilation produced a heavy stench of ammonia from the animals' urine.
- In the lower holds (aft) I found distressed cattle standing in a mixture of slurry and water which in places rose as high as 18 inches on our waders.

I later told the Captain of my findings. He showed little or no interest, so with my colleague I again went round the holds. We pulled animals back on their feet where they had fallen to the deck, made the pens as secure as we could and saw that food and water were given to them all. Finally, reeking strongly of smoke and ammonia, we returned to the pilot boat and went back to the harbour. Arrangements were made to have the ship towed into Fishguard.

I was then free to return to my base in Aberystwyth. In the next few hours the cattle were transferred to another ship, and I learned afterwards that they eventually reached Libya after a voyage lasting many more days than it should have done. A few days later, the fire-damaged hulk sank in the waters off Fishguard.

The episode was an eye-opener for me. Outside the merchant navy, few people have any idea of how live animals are carried on board a ship. The poor state of the pens on this particular cargo vessel, and the haphazard way the cattle were fed and watered, clearly showed that even minimum standards were not being enforced. If live animals must be sent by sea, then we need a vigilant international Inspectorate to make sure they are transported in a safe, humane manner. At present there are far too many loopholes for ruthless traders and shippers to exploit. At least within the Common Market countries, and preferably on a wider scale, we should be demanding much tighter legislation and a system of inspection that is internationally understood and respected.

Transit by air
The transportation of animals by air is a growing trade. Of those entering the UK, many are exotic animals and arrive after long flights from distant lands. Many die en route; some survive to end up in a zoo; others are destined for animal laboratories which use them for experimental purposes.

I want to look in particular at an export trade which does the British no credit at all. For many years, dealers and so-called international security companies have been supplying large numbers of dogs to serve abroad as guard dogs. One of the main client countries is Nigeria, and there is also a ready market in Malaysia.

The dogs are crated up at the dealers' establishments, then sent by road to airports such as East Midlands, Luton, Manston, Stansted and Gatwick. The conditions under which they are forced to travel are cramped and frightening. On arrival in a country such as Nigeria, many of the dogs are weakened or exhausted, and then must cope with an alien climate. Few survive longer than six months. The heat, disease, poor diet and low level of care are more than these poor animals can withstand.

The high mortality rate of the dogs does nothing to diminish the demand for them. I know of one dealer in the North of England who was asked to supply dogs at the rate of 400 per year. The security company he dealt with, which has offices in London, is no fly-by-night outfit.

In one particular contract the dealer undertook to supply 50 dogs for £5,500. He agreed not to sell any dog or dogs to West Africa except through that company. Initially, he would be supplied with 36 crates at the company's expense; thereafter he would be responsible for providing his own containers. The contract was valid for two years.

Correspondence between the two parties referred to the dealer's 'breeding farm'. In reality, there was no such farm. The dealer rounded up the number of dogs he required by placing advertisements in local newspapers. A typical ad. would read:

'WANTED Adult Alsatians, Dobermans, suitable to train for industrial police work. Telephone ...'

The wording has a broad appeal, as dealers of this type well know. It offers a convenient excuse for owners who want to get rid of their dog – but who want to do so with a clear conscience. Maybe the dog has become too 'keen' (the polite word for aggressive), or the owners were never able to cope with it in the first place, or they simply could not be bothered with it any more, or recognised that it was costing them too much in food and vet's bills. For some while they have been looking to offload the dog, without actually killing or dumping it, then along comes this very convenient get-out. 'Couldn't be better,' they think to themselves. 'After all, it's not going to be put down. It's going to become a police dog.'

Very few of the dogs supplied via such advertisements become police dogs. Their former owners could not really care less about that, and make little effort to find out what will happen to their animal. Once it is off their hands, their interest in it ceases.

These guard-dog dealers also call in at kennels which house stray dogs – or they get someone to call in for them – and offer to adopt or buy any suitable dogs that are available for rehoming. On the whole, I am glad to say, kennel managers are wise to these people and refuse to supply them.

It mattered little to that dealer in the North of England that he had no breeding farm or adequate kennels. He 'trained' his new dogs by chaining them up in a cellar, leaving them hungry and taunting them to make them vicious.

With a newspaper reporter I went to his so-called 'dog training centre', from which he also ran a company supplying security dogs. We pretended to be partners in a garage business and said we were looking for a dog to guard our premises. The dealer offered us a dog for £80, adding that he could sell the same dog abroad for double the price. He also gave us some advice about how to bend the law, including what to tell the police if they found the dog alone and uncontrolled. We listened, thanked him and left. A report subsequently appeared in the *Yorkshire Evening Post*, warning the public of this man's activities.

To me, one of the outstanding features of this trade in guard dogs for Nigeria and elsewhere is that it is so unnecessary. It is bad enough that any animal should be exploited in this way. That, however, is not the point of my argument. There is no need at all to crate up hundreds of dogs each year and fly them out to Nigeria, Singapore or wherever. If these countries invested in their own relatively small breeding stocks, they could breed their own animals and save themselves vast sums of money. Modern methods of artificial insemination would make it possible to improve the stock and countless animals would be spared the unnecessary suffering they undergo at present during the long hours of transportation. Many premature deaths would also be avoided, because the breeding stock would soon become better adapted to the hot local climate.

It is only the greed of the dealers that sustains this cruel trade. It is time the authorities woke up to what is going on and imposed effective curbs on the export of dogs. They should also take a careful look at the conditions under which all animals are sent alive to foreign countries, whether by land, sea or air.

Transit by road

The greatest volume of abuse occurs in the transit of farm animals for the meat trade. Very early in my career as an RSPCA Inspector, I worked with a colleague on an investigation into the export of calves to Europe. As part of our study we decided to follow a consignment of calves across the Channel and monitor the rest of their journey up to the point of delivery.

At Ostend, vehicles laden with live animals drove off the ferries and parked up on the quayside to await Customs clearance. It was summer and many of the trucks had to stand for long hours in blazing heat. The cries coming from the distressed and frightened calves after a five-hour sea crossing will live with me forever. When the trucks finally got going again, we followed them through Belgium, the Netherlands and into West Germany. The trucks continued eastwards, and at the border with East Germany we had to stop and turn back. By then the calves had been travelling for more than 18 hours and still had not reached their destination. When they did, they were to be slaughtered for veal.

Journeys such as this are inhumane and unnecessary. As I have already said, and no doubt will say many more times in the future, the avoidance of animal suffering must be given greater priority. If it were, a simple solution could soon be reached. The animals would be slaughtered in the UK and supplied to the customer in Europe as meat on the hook, delivered by refrigerated truck.

In many ways the operation of a single market economy in the EC will open up exciting new perspectives, but I am pessimistic about the benefits to animal welfare. As the trading boundaries in western Europe dissolve, we should be pressing our Government to impose a ban on the export of live animals for food. To many farmers throughout the Community this will be seen as a signal of liberation – a licence to send cattle and sheep to yet more distant destinations, trucking them anywhere from Wales to Greece or Spain, causing distress and suffering to vast numbers of livestock.

It is a thoroughly bad prospect, and one which our current legislation is ill-equipped to resist. British laws relating to the transportation of animals are not only puny, they are almost impossible to enforce.

In 1975 Parliament brought into being the Transit of Animals (Road and Rail) Order 1975. Article 10 of this Order made it a legal requirement to feed and water all animals travelling by road at intervals of not less than 12 hours. Then, in the Great British spirit of compromise, it undermined its authority by adding: 'or if the journey is completed within 15 hours of the last feed, it shall be sufficient to feed the animals immediately upon arrival at the destination.'

The Order is widely ignored. Drivers know that the police do not have the manpower available to monitor this kind of offence. Unless they do something quite blatant to draw attention to themselves, or get involved in an accident, they can be almost 100 per cent certain that their journey will be uninterrupted. Even if stopped, they can claim to have fed and watered the animals more recently than they have done, and will probably get away with it. To secure a conviction, investigators need to follow the driver for, in effect, his entire journey. No police force can spare even a single car crew for that period of time, nor would they want to send their officers far beyond their own region on a mission concerned with animal welfare.

As so often happens, it is left to animal welfare bodies to carry out these investigations. In 1978 I was involved in the first case brought before the courts under this Order. While investigating this particular case, I learned a great deal about the suffering caused to animals during such a journey. It is almost as though these animals ceased to exist as living things. Once loaded on a truck, it seems they have no more rights than a piece of furniture.

On many journeys, for example, animals are driven past a number of slaughterhouses. Why can we not do something to reduce the misery of these poor animals by making it a legal requirement that they be slaughtered as close as possible to the point of sale?

The fact is, such a requirement would break up an old network operated by farmers, dealers and auctioneers, who between them determine where animals are sold and taken for slaughter. It is my firm contention that they should not be allowed to get away with this any longer. Times have changed. In the minds of the majority of British people, animals deserve a new deal – one that respects their rights as living creatures which depend on man to feed and care for them.

A partial remedy would be to scrap the archaic cattle auctions that take place up and down the country and send those animals that have to be slaughtered direct from the farm to the nearest abattoir.

Turning again to the export trade, I would like to see a ban on the export of all live animals being sent for food. Under such a ban, it would be compulsory to ship all meat in carcase form.

Who would fail to benefit under such a system? Only the dealers who at present reckon to extract a higher price from their Continental customers for meat supplied on the hoof. We must also remember the by-products from these animals. There is a lucrative secondary trade in, for example, offal, hides which supply the leather industry, and even glue which is made from the hooves.

These markets would not disappear if an export ban were imposed. It would be up to British companies to enlarge their current capacity for handling these by-products. The benefits would then go to the British economy.

Such a proposal may not appeal to the EC authorities in Brussels, concerned as they are with harmonising national laws and trading conditions within the Community. I am aware of this and I respect their ideals, and the fact that they have a difficult job to do in uniting 12 nations into their concept of a single 'Europe Limited'.

However, I do not believe it is necessarily a sign of weakness to allow exceptions to a general rule. To those of us who are concerned about the future of animal welfare in Britain, it is important, no, *essential* that in some ways our status as an island be recognised as special. Like it or not, we in Britain are different. We cannot pretend that our transportation problems are the same as those of France, Germany or Italy. We are separated from Europe by seas which add at least three hours to journey times on even the shortest crossings, and six hours or more on most of the others.

To ferry animals to Europe in less than 12 hours is therefore difficult, if not impossible, from most starting points in the UK. We now have enough experience to know that these long-drawn-out journeys to Europe, including an often turbulent sea crossing, are the cause of more distress and suffering to our farm animals than any other type of journey. Surely, today, that is reason enough to put a stop to them. The advent of the Channel Tunnel will, in my opinion, do little to help the situation.

What really annoys me is that we have made so little progress since the Order became law. If we had spent those years working towards a ban on the export of live animals, we would be far better equipped to face the next wave of chaos which is bound to arrive with the Single European Market.

We have been apathetic for too long. Shall we now find that we have left it too late?

ZOOS AND CIRCUSES

Recently the media have given a lot of coverage to the plight of zoos. Many have experienced falling numbers of visitors.

I have never been a great supporter of zoos, and the problems of dealing with the closure of Knaresborough Zoo has left me with bitter memories. Faced with the problem of finding homes for some 300 animals and being successful in 294 cases, I was nonetheless forced to concede that for six animals there was nothing I could do but have them humanely destroyed. This type of action is not, nor ever was, my aim in life. But the fact is that today, there are far too many of certain types of animals to go around the remaining zoos in this country.

It is very wrong in my opinion to cage up an animal in an enclosure, when that animal, in the wild, would travel many miles in a day. To use as an excuse the fact that these animals are born in captivity is nonsense.

Circus animals face an even worse fate. At least the zoo animal is in a static position and has a 'home'. The poor circus animal is confined to a travelling cage for most of the year and only let out to perform tricks which are undignified to such majestic animals as an elephant or tiger.

EXPERIMENTS AND VIVISECTION

The definition in the dictionary I use of the word vivisection is 'the act or practice of performing experiments on living animals, involving cutting into or dissecting the body'. In today's modern world of computers and culture growth, I can see no reason for this activity to take place. Surely over the years, enough information has been gleaned about all animals and how their bodies function without having to carry on this disgusting practice.

In a northern university in June 1982 and 1983, cats were mounted on spinal frames and part of the spinal cord exposed. Certain nerves, including one from the genitals, were electrically stimulated and the effects observed. This vivisection was financed by the Medical Research Council.

I am pleased to say that many schools and colleges no longer use animals for experiments. I know that this has come as quite a relief to many young students who did not want to commit this type of act. In the past if they did not, they would have failed their exams.

It is worth remembering that at any given moment, 100,000 experiments are being carried out on animals around the world.

ANIMALS IN THE LABORATORY

On February 12th 1992, an overwhelming majority of MEPs voted to stop the testing of toiletries and cosmetics on animals. If the European Ministers can be persuaded to support this ban there would be three important consequences. Firstly, a ban on the marketing of products containing ingredients tested on animals could be in place within two years; secondly, a central European inventory of ingredients used in cosmetics could be compiled, listing the Safety Tests undertaken on each substance and any experiments carried out on animals – at present 8,000 ingredients have been approved and new ones will only be approved if they have *not* been tested on animals. Thirdly, details of ingredients would appear on the label or leaflet when an item is sold.

I want to give my own views on the use of animals for scientific experiments. Many of the experiments conducted today are unnecessary and that the present controls on them need tightening. It would be a duty of my proposed Ministry to bring this about.

Let us consider the cosmetics industry. This is an area which worries me since it is wholly driven by commercial interests. It is time the big companies accepted that it is no longer necessary to experiment on animals simply to create new ranges of shampoos, soaps or make-up. We have enough of these already. To make more is greedy and irresponsible. If the rage for novelty must be satisfied, companies such as The Body Shop have shown that plenty of other, natural sources can be tapped. The kind of laboratory work which is devoted to developing and testing new cosmetic products could be halted today – with no loss to humanity.

The drugs industry also gives me cause for concern. I believe that we do not need the present variety of similar drugs performing the same function to cope with the world's health problems. The lists of approved drugs could be drastically trimmed, and animal experiments could be a thing of the past.

Let me give an example: there is a particular test called the LD50 test. 'LD' stands for Lethal Dose. The test is used to assess the safety or toxicity of a substance. In the laboratory, scientists administer various concentrations of the substance to different groups of animals. The aim is to discover which concentration is lethal to 50 per cent of the test group.

At present this test is a Government safety requirement. Over the years it has become a standard way to evaluate toxicity in drugs, food additives, agricultural chemicals and other consumer products. Large numbers of test animals are thus doomed to die, killed either by the toxicity of the substance or by the sheer physical effects of force-feeding them with it.

The RSPCA, through its Committee for the Reform of Animal Experimentation (CRAE), is campaigning for the Home Office to ban this method of testing. Its own studies show that the test is in many instances misleading, and scientifically invalid in others. It is expensive to carry out and, most important of all, causes pain and distress to the test animals.

The CRAE urges that other methods be found and encouraged, and that toxicity data should be pooled to cut down on the number of animals used for tests. The CRAE also says that too many animals are used per test. From a statistical point of view, equally satisfactory results could be achieved by using fewer animals.

The LD50 test highlights a distressing problem. Research companies use it because the Government says it is necessary. They no longer question its accuracy or true usefulness, but apply it because their clients need to satisfy the legislative requirements of this country and others to which their products may be exported. The test, in essence, has no more value than a rubber stamp on a document. It is a passport to making money. Because of it, thousands of animals suffer pain, distress and early death.

The question facing animal welfare groups is this. How do you go about changing the Government's mind about the LD50 and other unnecessary tests? Do you proceed carefully, logically and moderately to point out, using the evidence of your own research, that such a test is largely worthless and always cruel? Or do you go for the terrorist approach, breaking into buildings and placing bombs where they can injure men, women and children who have nothing to do with experiments carried out on animals?

I am in no doubt that the Animal Liberation terrorists have got it badly wrong. Wherever they go, they alienate and divide, and cause wanton damage to people and property. It is no way to achieve reform in such a delicate field as animal welfare.

To go around blowing up a department store because it sells fur coats is not the way to win sympathy and support. The actions of the violent fringe run directly counter to the methods and objectives of the major charities, and in the long run it is the charities who suffer most because the public confuses one with the other, turns its back on them and refuses to give.

ANIMAL RIGHTS TERRORISM
Campaigners for animal rights, whether they belong to one of the principal charities or to a small private group, usually set out with

the best of intentions. Many of those who found their own group are disillusioned members of bigger societies. They become frustrated by the way their governing body controls the members' activities. They feel that more should be done on a specific issue or issues, and with a number of like-minded people form their own breakaway faction.

Most small groups concentrate on one issue. If it is animal experiments, they arrange outings to picket laboratories in their area. This is perfectly legitimate, provided it is done peacefully. Another group may object chiefly to animals being used to perform in circuses. You find them protesting outside circus tents, handing out leaflets to try and persuade people not to attend performances. Again they are entitled to do this so long as they stick to peaceful means.

As a group they often meet at a member's house, then go out to a pub afterwards to socialise and enjoy each other's company. This is when they are most vulnerable to infiltrators.

On the fringe of the animal welfare groups, there are sinister individuals constantly on the lookout for a way to advance their own, far from peaceful aims. To secure themselves a cover of respectability, they join a legitimate group and then, quietly and expertly, introduce their own friends to it.

In a short time, they take control of the peaceful group, and its funds, and set about organising their own programme of havoc and destruction. Where once, in the old group, people campaigned against man's inhumanity to animals, the new programme is dominated by a very different concept: man's inhumanity to man. The animals, in effect, become bystanders in a guerrilla campaign in which the targets are people, and the means of attack are violent and life-threatening.

These people are a perplexing mixture of animal-rights fanatics and out-and-out criminals who care nothing for animals but use the name of an animal protection group as a shelter while they wreak their private revenge on society.

In the mid-'80s three men were jailed for four years after pleading guilty to taking part in a reign of terror against businesses and organisations which they claimed were cruel to animals. They attacked a number of properties with fire bombs, etching fluids, crossbows and hammers. In one attack they used a miniature fire bomb, contained in a cigarette packet, to cause more than £200,000 of damage to a large department store.

Within a few years the three were free and recruiting members for their new 'animal protection group'. They claimed to be working alongside the RSPCA and an established and respected Badger Group, but neither wanted to have anything to do with them.

'Any involvement with this new group would jeopardise all our work,' said a spokesman for the Badger Group. 'The three men have been to prison for the fanatical way they pursued animal rights and we simply do not want to be associated with such views.'

In Court the men had been described to the Judge as 'common soldiers' in the Animal Liberation Front. The paramilitary term gives a flavour of their shady, undercover methods.

Like the misguided enthusiasts of the dog-fighting world, many members of the ALF live outside the law and seem to delight in producing subversive underground publications. In their news-sheets they publish lists of arrests made of their members and appeal for funds to help with their defence.

Applicants to join the Animal Liberation Front are carefully screened. Recent publicity has made them aware that they too are vulnerable to infiltration, and they are very guarded about whom they will allow to join their ranks.

I have obtained a copy of their Code of Practice and reproduce its terms below. They may come as a shock to anyone who thinks that animal welfare is mainly to do with actually looking after animals and seeing that they are well cared for.

A. NEW MEMBERS
1. Any prospective member of the group will be allocated a task to be performed by him or herself single-handedly. Advice and equipment necessary for completion of that task will be provided by the group.

Memberships of the group will be considered by the group if:
> **A.** The candidate successfully completes the task without detection, or

B. The candidate is caught and charged and can prove to the group's satisfaction THAT

– he or she was caught due to no fault of his or her own.

– he or she has given no written or verbal statement to the police incriminating him or herself or any other person.

If he or she fails to complete his or her task and is not caught, then he or she will be required to furnish an explanation to the group. If the group is satisfied with the explanation given, then he or she will be allocated another task and the same conditions will apply.

2. The group reserves the right to allocate as many tasks as they see fit to any person before giving membership to that person.

3. Any prospective member who can furnish evidence of having been charged with a relevant offence within the previous six months may be considered for exemption from the procedure outlined in No.1 above, subject to the conditions in 1B above.

4. Any prospective member will be given the codes relating to security at the time of his or her first application for membership. Membership will not be given to any person who subsequently contravenes those codes.

B. SECURITY

1. No member is to discuss group activities in any form whatsoever in any public place, except those designated as reasonably safe by the group.

2. No member is to discuss group activities in any form whatsoever with any person or persons except the following:

A. Other group members.

B. Any person specially authorised by the group, e.g. steady girl/boyfriends, wives, recognised contacts from other groups, etc.

3. Members must exercise caution at all times when communicating by telephone or by post. Details of any group activities must be only communicated by word of mouth. Except apart from the above.

C. LEGAL

1. A solicitor of the group's choice must be made available as soon as possible to any person arrested on or as a result of any of the group's activities. Account of this must be made at the planning stage of any of the group's activities.

D. PERSONAL RESPONSIBILITY
During a group activity a reasonable amount of assistance must be given to any person engaged upon that activity who is in difficulty unless he or she specifically declines it. However the group considers that it is pointless for activists to be arrested needlessly, so special account must be taken of this.

E. FINANCES
1. A full (so far as security considerations will allow) record of the group's finances must be kept and be available for inspection by any group member on demand.
2. Any person handling cheques or cash to give full details of any transactions to the group.

F. MEDIA
Any communication to the media (inc ALFSG) concerning the group's activities to be approved by the group before hand.

G. CONTACT WITH OTHER GROUPS
Any person contacting other groups to report back giving full details to the group.

H. DIET
All members to be vegan or vegetarian.

I. DISCIPLINE
1. Any member found acting in contravention to the above will be liable to disciplinary action by the group. Persistent offenders will be liable to suspension or expulsion from the group.
2. Any person giving a statement to the police incriminating him/ herself will be liable to disciplinary action by the group.
3. Any person giving a statement to the police incriminating any person other than him/herself will be expelled without exception.

At every step the compilers of the Code betray themselves. The obsessive secrecy, the initiation 'task' which is equivalent to 'a relevant offence', the security codes, the repeated threats of 'disciplinary action', the irrational fear of both the media and the police all add up to show that it is inconceivable that any member of the Animal Liberation Front puts the cause of animals first. They are far too interested in playing their own secret games, and winning victories in their little war on society. We need to be more wary of these people and their violent methods. The real problems of animal welfare are much more complicated and require sensitive handling if we are to make real progress.

THE FRAMEWORK AND THE FLAWS

THE CURRENT LEGAL FRAMEWORK

Looking back over two hundred years of history, it is clear that the most successful campaigners for animal rights were not blinkered extremists but committed humanitarians. One of the first was a wealthy Dublin-born MP, Richard Martin. His battles to push Bills through Parliament that would give animals a better deal earned him the nickname 'Humanity Dick'. After many years of defeat, he succeeded with a Bill that gave some protection to the cow, ox, heifer, steer and other cattle, the horse and sheep.

Martin's Bill made it an offence for someone having charge or custody of animals belonging to other persons, to wantonly beat, abuse or ill-treat them. That still left people free to do as they liked with their own animals, but it was a good step forward. The Bill received the Royal Assent on 22 July 1822.

Since that date there have been all sorts of new Bills and amendments to old ones, until today we have a dense and confusing hotch-potch of legislation that only an expert can understand. We badly need an enlightened Government to draw all these laws together, and to streamline and bring them up to date.

Our laws relating to animals are in chaos. There is no single body responsible for administering them. No wonder people are confused. Let me briefly explain how the law stands at present. There are three basic divisions of responsibility:

- The laws governing **cruelty to animals**, and the penalties for **causing unnecessary suffering**. These are administered by the Courts. Each case, according to its severity, is heard before Magistrates, or a Judge in the Crown Court.
- The laws which cover the **licensing** of boarding, breeding and riding establishments, zoos, circuses, wildlife parks, dangerous wild animals and pet shops. These are the

responsibility of the local authority; in other words, your district council.
- The laws governing **farm animals** and their welfare. These are the responsibility of the Ministry of Agriculture, Fisheries and Food.

So much for the types of legislation dealing with animals. If any law is to work, however, it needs to be enforced. To care for our animals, to prevent cruelty and suffering, to make sure breeders and dealers take out proper licenses, there should be an official, Government-run Inspectorate working in parallel with the police force.

Now let us look in greater detail at these three divisions of the law and how each is applied.

CRUELTY TO ANIMALS

It is in theory the duty of the police to investigate and prosecute cases of cruelty. In practice, they will freely admit that they do not have the time to do so. Their first priority is to deal with crimes against people, and that is more than enough for them.

There is a political side to their predicament. The police must be seen at all times to put people first. Think what would happen if it came to light that while someone was being raped or mugged, the police were away questioning a man about why he did not feed his dog. There would be a public outcry, and I for one would sympathise with any police force which found itself in such a corner.

The laws covering animal welfare are widespread and complicated. Few police officers understand, for example, the intricacies of 'causing unnecessary suffering to an animal'. Although, officially, police officers are charged by Parliament with upholding the cruelty laws, in practice they ask their local RSPCA officer to make the investigation and, if necessary, to bring a case before the Magistrates.

This is unfair. The RSPCA Inspector has no more power in law than a normal citizen and cannot legally compel anyone to answer any question put to them. Far too much is expected from this uniformed body. Furthermore as the RSPCA has no official standing in the legislative framework of this country, such cases have to be brought as private prosecutions, and must be paid for out of the

Society's funds. Unless the case is brought by the police, the Government contributes nothing.

Many RSPCA officers attend court more times in a year than a police officer will do in his whole career. In this book you will find numerous examples of cases which the RSPCA dealt with on behalf of the police. They cover all kinds of offences, among them dog-fighting, badger-baiting and cruelty to domestic pets.

LICENSING

Much the same applies to the laws which cover animals breeders, zoos, pet shop owners, and so on. These, as I have said, are in the hands of the local authority. The actual work is delegated to the councils' Environmental Health Officers.

They too have so many different problems to deal with in their sphere of operations, that they rarely find time to keep individual breeders, dealers, pet shop owners and all the others up to the various marks laid down by the law. Instead they rely on the RSPCA and other charities to report to them and initiate court actions.

FARM ANIMALS

The Ministry of Agriculture, Fisheries and Food is a vast organisation with a correspondingly vast number of powers. Of all the agencies which have responsibility for animal welfare, it is, in my opinion, the least effective. It is conspicuously weak when dealing with the welfare of farm animals.

Like the other agencies it is without doubt understaffed, but even in the most blatant cases of cruelty to farm animals its officers show a marked reluctance to bring farmers before the courts. I have been involved in too many cases where I have called out a Ministry Vet who has been unwilling or reluctant to attend, and who then found there was no case of cruelty. At further cost to charity funds, I then had to summon a private vet to deal with the situation.

I have also been in court on numerous occasions when the Ministry Vet, originally called out by me, opted to give evidence in support of the defence. In every such case, I am pleased to say, justice eventually prevailed and the quality of the Ministry Vet's evidence was seen to be less than adequate.

One explanation for the unpredictable standards of Ministry

Vets is that their loyalties often appear divided. If the Ministries of Food and Agriculture were separated, this would no doubt sharpen their vision, which so often fails to be objective. All the same, it is my view that no veterinary surgeon, no matter who employs him, should be prepared to condone the suffering of any animal whatsoever.

LEGISLATIVE CHAOS

The entire structure of legislation, if you can call it a structure, is flawed from top to bottom. It is absurd that most of the prosecutions brought before the courts today are made under the Protection of Animals Act of 1911.

It is ridiculous to continue tacking bits and pieces on to an Act of Parliament which was written for society as it was 80 years ago. In those days, human rights were in a primitive state, unrecognisable and unacceptable by the standards of today. As for attitudes towards animals, they came in a very poor second. The time has come to abandon our antiquated systems and make a fresh start. In the interests of all animals – sheep, cattle, pigs, horses, dogs, cats and all pets and wild animals held in captivity in this country – we urgently need a single Government ministry to supervise their welfare and enforce relevant legislation, one that is properly staffed and headed by a Government Minister.

THE LAW IN PRACTICE

To some extent problems arise because of currently held attitudes. Many magistrates and solicitors do not treat cases of animal cruelty as seriously as they should. The penalties are there for magistrates to apply, but in far too many cases that I have come across they decline to use them.

The penalties

The penalties for offences committed in England and Wales are defined in most cases by The Standard Scale of Fines laid down by Parliament. This 'standard scale' dictates the maximum amount that an adult can be fined on conviction of a summary offence. For example, under the Protection of Animals Act 1911, a person convicted of causing unnecessary suffering to an animal faces a fine within Level 5 (up to £2,000). In addition, the offender could also be sent to prison. At the time of writing, the levels are as follows:

Level 1	£50
Level 2	£100
Level 3	£400
Level 4	£1,000
Level 5	£2,000

These punishments demonstrate how seriously cases of cruelty to animals should be taken. Why else would they be available to magistrates and judges?

Far too often, however, the punishment fails to fit the crime. This is not only unjust, it is very discouraging to all those who work so hard to bring cases before the magistrates.

At present the odds are stacked against the justice-seekers. To bring a case to court is often a nightmarish procedure. The workings of the law are cumbersome and ineffective, and the costs involved are potentially ruinous. Let us look at these two matters separately.

BRINGING A CASE TO COURT

Most cases of cruelty to animals are brought as private prosecutions by charities, such as the RSPCA, the RSPB and the Horses and Ponies Protection Society. Because of their private nature, they are automatically given a low priority. In some areas private prosecutions are heard only weekly or monthly.

Very seldom is a case heard at the first hearing. More often than not, the defendant does not appear and arrangements have to be made to serve a personal summons.

Even after this has been done, the case may still not go ahead. There are two principal reasons for this:

- The summons has not been served. Police seem to give these matters a low priority, to be got round to when they feel they have the time.

- The summons is served but the defendant decides not to turn up in court. A warrant may then be requested for his arrest. Finally the defendant does appear, and pleads 'not guilty'. The case is then adjourned and another date is set. Meanwhile the defendant almost invariably goes home free, even though the charges against him may be serious.

What happens next? Sometimes, nothing happens. I was in court on one occasion when the defendant was a woman who had been served with a warrant for her arrest after failing to attend court, despite being personally served with a summons. She was released by the Magistrate to appear in one week's time to answer the serious charges against her. To this day she has not appeared. Surely, people such as this who show total disregard for the law should not be allowed to go free until those charges have been heard.

All these delays are expensive both in time and money. We need also to think of any animals involved which have to be specially looked after until the court decides whether or not to return them to the owner. Even if it is clear that the animal must not be returned to the defendant, nothing can be done about finding a new owner until the court has reached its verdict. Delays can go on for months, more than a year in some cases, causing further unnecessary distress to the animal.

COURT CASES: THE COST
The costs of bringing a private prosecution before the magistrates have to be borne by the individual or society bringing the case. These costs can be daunting. They have to include:
- Vet's report and statement.
- Veterinary fees for treating the animal(s).
- Vet's attendance in court.
- Boarding fees for the animal.
- Appointing a solicitor to conduct the case.
- Solicitor's fees for appearing in court.
- The administrative costs of the person or body bringing the case – these could include office expenses, witness fees, travel costs, time and so on.

The high costs of a court action can in practice deter a charity or individual from bringing a case to court. This should not happen, but if the funds are low, then hard commercial considerations must be taken into account.

Even when the case is won, those bringing the case to court may still lose out financially. If there is a conviction, the law provides for costs to be awarded against the defendant. However, these costs are seldom recovered in full.

By in practice penalising those who bring court cases, the law commits a double injustice. The authorities conveniently forget that the reason the charity or individual got involved in the first place is because the law enforcement agencies of this country are unable to provide animals with the protection that is their right.

FLAWS IN THE SYSTEM

ANTIQUATED LEGISLATION

Antiquated legislation and legal anomalies exist by the score. You need only to read what I said earlier on Wild Birds to see how complicated our laws have become. I will give another example now concerning horses. Under the Protection of Animals Act 1911, an owner may be prosecuted for causing unnecessary suffering to a horse, and this, 80 years later, is what we still seek to prove when bringing a case to court. Recently an amendment to the Act was introduced which people generally hailed as a great step forward. This made it an offence to 'tether any horse, ass or mule under such conditions or in such a manner as to cause that animal unnecessary suffering'.

To me, this amendment is not worth the paper it is written on. It offers nothing that was not already covered by the original Act. I only mention it here because I feel an important opportunity was missed to clarify the obligations of people owning horses. If the amendment had made it an offence, for example, to tether a horse where it had no access to water, or protection from severe weather, or where other specific conditions were not observed, then we might have got somewhere. The law could have been changed to impose tougher responsibilities on horse owners, with obvious benefits to the horses themselves.

The law is still too slack and needs to be tightened. We should also be looking at the reasons why so many horses are abused in this way. In the end, it is too easy to acquire a horse or pony. They are too cheap to buy, and there are too many of them. As with the puppy farmers we should be trying to make the breeders reduce their output. Perhaps there should be some form of quota system which limits the number of horses that can be put on the market in a given year. Each licensed breeder could be allocated a maximum share in that quota, according to the size and standard of his premises, and would be penalised with a heavy fine for exceeding his share.

The breeders would undoubtedly wail and gnash their teeth at the prospect of further legal restraints. They would, however, have the necessary respect for a system of penalties which aimed at the horse trader's most vulnerable spot – his wallet.

LEGAL ANOMALIES

For an example of an anomaly, take squirrels. The red squirrel is a protected species and must not be touched. The grey squirrel is the opposite – classified as vermin. If you come across an injured grey squirrel, technically you should not care for it. That is an offence. According to the law, you should kill it. It makes no sense to protect one type of squirrel and discriminate against another. But the law states, in effect, that you cannot be cruel to a wild animal unless it is captive or protected – as, for instance, badgers and red squirrels.

I had a case where a 16-year-old boy had stunned a grey squirrel in a wood. He then trapped it in a small pen made of loose bricks and tormented the animal by throwing more stones at its head. The squirrel was badly dazed when we rescued it and died five days later. A post-mortem showed it had suffered damage to the brain.

I wanted to bring a case against the boy but our lawyers were doubtful. Squirrels are wild animals, they said, and we should have to prove that this one was captive during the period when the boy exercised what the law calls 'acts of dominion' over it.

We managed to do this, but at the time there was no certainty that we would win. The Magistrates accepted our argument that the boy had first maimed the animal by hitting it with a stone. While it was dazed and incapable of escaping, he had imprisoned it in the pen, and also used a piece of wood to cover the top of the pen. The animal was therefore in a state of captivity when he caused it further injuries from which it died.

The boy was found guilty and fined. I hoped we had deterred him from doing this kind of thing again, and the publicity surrounding the case was a useful warning to others. What concerned me, though, was that many other types of cruelty would still go unpunished. If the boy had knocked the squirrel out of a tree with a stone, for example, that would not count as cruelty. I think that is nonsense. Morally, it cannot be justified.

On St Valentine's Day 1992, Kevin McNamara introduced a Private Member's Bill, the 'Wild Mammals (Protection) Bill'. In this bill, the MP for Hull North tried to provide protection for wild mammals not already protected by law. His bill would have brought to an end snaring and such acts of violence as playing football with a live hedgehog. The bill was defeated by eight votes. The problem was, in my opinion, that when the bill was debated, fox-hunting was taken as its main issue by its opponents. Although public opinion seems to be very much against fox-hunting, there are, it appears, still many members of Parliament who, for whatever reason, feel that it should continue.

Because of this fox-hunting issue, some MPs are quite happy to allow snaring and other forms of animal suffering to continue. I sincerely hope that in a future Parliament this issue will be raised again. Only eight votes stopped the bill from proceeding to its second reading. Who knows, perhaps the new Parliament might have a few more humane members.

THE COST TO THE NATION
Flaws in the current system cost all of us a great deal of money. Take the huge sums needlessly spent on stray dogs.

Outside the home, the dog has a tarnished image, seen by many people as dirty, diseased and dangerous. This sounds a rather emotional view. It has been partly formed by media pressure, with over-excited TV debates and banner headlines which inflate and distort. Nevertheless, we are faced with an acute dog problem.

Quite simply, there are too many dogs in Britain today, and far too many of these are stray dogs. A stray dog, by the usual definition, is one not under his owner's control. This includes dogs which have temporarily escaped from the home, but in the main it refers to dogs which are permanently on the loose, usually because their owners have lost interest in them or cannot afford to feed them. To their number we need to add the 'latchkey' dogs which are turned out of their homes each day when their owners go out.

Dogs are pack animals, and very soon they form gangs. Together they cause havoc on housing estates and in public parks. They break into school playgrounds, terrifying and injuring children. Head teachers are rightly angry about this. When I tell them that the dog wardens are hopelessly understaffed to prevent these attacks, they are understandably unimpressed.

Wherever these dogs go, they intimidate and frighten people, making them afraid to go out. In their packs they look dangerous, unpredictable, wolf-like. People have read enough in their newspapers lately about 'killer dogs'. The last thing they want is to find what looks like a pack of them living on their doorstep.

On the 1st of April 1992, the responsibility for stray dogs passed, by virtue of the Environmental Protection Act of 1990, from the police to the local authorities. This act tells local authorities that they have a duty to appoint an officer to collect and deal with strays and to enforce the existing collar and tag legislation under the 1930 Control of Dogs Order. The Government has told local authorities that they may charge a £25 reclaim fee on top of any boarding and other charges for the keep of the stray dog. The new act also addresses the issue of ownership of stray dogs. As from 1 April 1992, if a dog has not been reclaimed after seven days, the ownership of that dog automatically transfers to the new owner.

But whoever is responsible, dealing with stray dogs has now become a vast social problem. The Government has been slow to recognise this, but, as we shall see, the figures speak for themselves. Meanwhile, the politicians do little more than make speeches about the problem of strays, then stand back and hope that charities such as the RSPCA will take over and somehow make it go away.

What the Government fails to realise, or refuses to accept, is that this is no temporary nuisance but a long-lasting issue. The stray-dog population is now so large that it will not even be held in check, let alone reduced, until the problem is faced up to and met with adequate resources of public money and manpower. It is no good hoping that the present thinly scattered force of dog wardens can cope. They are over-stretched dealing with the symptoms of the problem. We must now get to grips with the cause.

If we look at the statistics, the scale of the problem is quickly revealed. In Britain today there are an estimated 8 million dogs and I believe that there are many more. In Leeds alone, which has a population of 500,000 people, there are more than 10,000 stray dogs at any one time. The cost to you and me of supporting all these stray dogs nationwide is now something like £77 million per year. To me that is a dreadful waste. I will show you how the total is arrived at. The figures come from a study carried out by the London School of Economics.

- In 1986, 240,000 dogs were officially registered as strays. Of these, 90,000 were destroyed.
- The cost of boarding 150,000 dogs at an average of £2.10 per day came to £2,205,000.
- The cost of destroying 90,000 dogs, at £8 per dog, came to £720,000.

If that average figure seems high, it is reached because many organisations are involved, together with individuals such as vets, and they charge commercial rates for what they do. What is more, this figure is likely to increase substantially in future because the RSPCA has plans to move away from destroying healthy animals by the mid-1990s.

- The total cost of boarding and destroying stray dogs, excluding police time, was therefore £2,925,000.
- Dogs were involved in 54,000 road accidents in 1988. The cost of this was £50 million, divided chiefly between the cost of insurance claims, police time and calling out emergency services.
- In 1987, dogs were involved in 1,069 accidents in which people were injured. The cost to the National Health Service of treating them was £17 million.
- The annual cost in 1988 to the NHS for the treatment of in-patients suffering from dog bites or dog-borne diseases was £875,000.
- The annual cost in 1988 to the National Health Service for accident and emergency services called to treat injuries directly caused by dogs was £5 million.
- The annual cost of injuries to or death of 10,000 farm animals caused through attacks by uncontrolled dogs was £1 million.
- The total of all these costs is £76,800,000.

That is a staggering sum. Just think what much-needed services the Government could buy with that kind of money – or even half of it. It would certainly more than help fund a dog registration scheme – a theme I shall return to shortly.

WHY WE NEED A MODERN SYSTEM

While animal welfare organisations do all they can to see that our animal laws are enforced, they face an unending uphill struggle. Laws grow more complicated with every addition and amendment stuck on to them, and it is becoming increasingly difficult for any unofficial, underfunded private body to keep up with the changes.

In particular, they cannot afford the equipment for the tape and video interviews which will soon become standard procedure. If they were part of a Government-funded Inspectorate, they could demand – and get – much more. They would have to be given appropriate powers and the equipment that goes with them, including up-to-date interview rooms, together with sufficient staff to operate them under the correct procedures.

Too often in the past, animal welfare organisations have had to work on their own, and the evidence they produced has had no more force than the words of the defendant. Where there is more than one defendant, the investigator's word is outnumbered by the denials of the other side, making it extremely difficult to secure a conviction. Today there is more pressure than ever to substantiate evidence.

There will always be a role for the RSPCA to play. It is the one it was originally founded to do – to prevent cruelty to animals. But policing the nation's animals, and more to the point their owners, is not an appropriate job for a modest charitable organisation, however dedicated its workers may be.

Let me sum up with three points:
- Laws protecting animals are on the statute books already, but they are not properly enforced in the courts.

- Animal laws need a drastic overhaul to simplify and bring them up to date.

- The job of tracking down offenders should be given to a specially trained, Government-funded Inspectorate.

MY SOLUTIONS

WANTED: A MINISTER FOR ANIMALS

Imagine this. The ruling Government appoints a Minister for Animals. After he has been in office for some weeks, Opposition MPs begin to ask questions in the House:

'Does the Minister realise that 90,000 dogs have to be put down every year, and that the cost to the nation of dealing with stray dogs is now running at £77 million per year? How does he propose to deal with these urgent matters?' And:

'Does the Minister realise that dog-fighting and badger-baiting are more widespread now than they have been for the last 50 years? How does he propose to clamp down on these repellent so-called sports?'

I can think of at least a dozen equally embarrassing questions for the new Minister, arising from problems which already exist, here and now, in our homes and on our roads, on farms and in open countryside throughout the land. It is a scandal that we have no appropriate Minister to deal with these pressing questions. If we did, one thing is certain. He would not be able to sweep them aside, as our present, fragmented bunch of administrators do. The press, and public opinion, would not allow that to happen.

A NEW DEAL FOR ANIMALS

Those of us who care for animals have a duty to prevent cruelty to *all* animals. We can, and should, campaign to change unjust laws. We must be careful, though, to do this in a civilised, moderate way.

My proposal is that we should work towards setting up a single Government department – a Ministry for Animals. It would be completely separate from the Ministry of Agriculture, Fisheries and Food, and would take over that ministry's powers in relation to farm animals.

The new Ministry would be responsible for all branches of animal welfare. It would have wide powers of inspection, from pet shops to farms, from performing animals to zoos. It would monitor the import and export of animals, the registration of all boarding, breeding and riding establishments. It would set up and administer a national dog registration scheme.

Once all these duties were under the control of a single department, millions of pounds would be saved compared with the sums we spend under the present fragmented system. In due course all the laws relating to animals would be rationalised, brought up to date and made more understandable. The benefits would be tremendous. At last we would have a cohesive means to safeguard the rights and welfare of all animals.

We should also be better equipped to deal with that body of dangerous extremists who have given such a bad name to the cause of animal rights, such as the Animal Liberation Front and similar groups. In recent years they have caused enormous damage and loss of public sympathy, not only for themselves but for the important work of mainstream, moderate groups who seek reforms through peaceful means.

Below are just some of the duties which Ministry Inspectors would be required to carry out:

- **Experiments on Animals**. Regular checks on experimental laboratories, questioning not only the way they are run but also whether their work is necessary.
- **Transit of Animals**. Regular road checks on vehicles transporting animals, chiefly to slaughterhouses and dealers. Compulsory inspection of all animals in transit at railway stations and haulage depots.
- **Boarding and Breeding Establishments**. Regular monitoring of zoos, pet shops, and all boarding and breeding establishments, to enforce the current standards and then raise them to higher levels.
- **Cattle Markets and Horse Sales**. Regular attendance to monitor how farmers and breeders bring their animals to market.
- **Dog Registration Scheme**. The setting up and running of a

national scheme which will deal with stray dogs and negligent owners.
- **Anti-Rabies Patrol**. This would be a special squad to guard against the illegal importation of animals which would operate at ports and airports. Monitoring of the Channel Tunnel would be a permanent top priority.
- **Education Programme**. The presentation of a multi-media programme, combined with regular visits to schools, hospitals, and so on, to teach the proper care of all animals, especially domestic pets.

There is nothing particularly new or radical about any of those schemes. Many of them have been around for years. Now is the time – for the first time – to implement them properly, backed by a single, professional, Government-funded organisation. I am convinced that this is the only way forward.

Minister, where are you?

REMEDIES TO THE DOG PROBLEM

As I have indicated earlier, the existence of far too many dogs in this country causes problems for all of us and is one of the most pressing animal issues requiring resolution. I have three proposals for regaining control over our dog population. The first deals with puppy farmers.

BAN THE PUPPY FARMERS

The time has come to clamp down on inferior dog-breeding establishments. We need higher licensing standards, supported by some kind of quota system, to bring down the number of kennel-bred dogs which arrive on the market each year.

I fully respect the work done by dedicated, legitimate breeders. At their best, they breed to perpetuate the line and to enter their dogs at shows. They respect their bitches and only sell the surplus puppies in their litters. They too ought to look carefully at the number of dogs they breed each year, but my principal target is the large number of illegitimate breeders. They are the people we must stop – the people who force their bitches to produce litter after litter of puppies, so they can line their own pockets. This method of breeding is indiscriminate and uncaring. If we can curb the activities of the puppy farmers, the number of dogs being offered for sale through dealers and pet shops would fall significantly.

NEUTERING

The cross-bred dog, our friend the mongrel, is a different problem. In no way would I wish to see the cross-bred dog disappear from our lives. The 'Heinz-57' dog has many good points and can make a wonderful companion. The trouble is, he always breeds when and where he can, and it is very difficult to stop him. The same applies, of course, to the thoroughbred puppy once he is settled in his new home and begins to grow up and mature.

Everyone I meet seems to have at least one story about a dog who is determined to defy his owner's efforts to keep him from mating with the bitch of his fancy. At such moments in his life, no fence is too high for the amorous dog, no wall can keep him out. I have even heard of a mating which took place through a chain-link fence.

While I sympathise with this dog's desires, we must do more to prevent him from achieving them. The answer lies in educating owners to neuter their dogs and bitches. Some, of course, already acknowledge this responsibility and see that it is carried out. Many more, however, although they seem prepared to have their dog neutered, are deterred by the cost.

They should not be. The cost of neutering is a tiny investment when set beside all the other expenses of feeding, maintenance and the occasional trip to the vet incurred during a dog's life. Only when many more people accept that neutering is a social duty, will we succeed in containing the puppy population.

REGISTRATION

All dogs and their owners should be registered. It is the only way to make owners accountable for their dogs.

Already in our cities people are afraid to take their dog for a walk in case a stray dog or a pack of strays attacks them. I don't blame the dogs concerned; it is not their fault. I blame their original owners who dump their dogs or turn them loose when they go out for the day.

There are many cases of people going on holiday and leaving

their dog to fend for itself on the streets. This is intolerable. They should be prosecuted for failing to provide necessary care and attention for the animal. However, without a registration scheme, ownership cannot be proved if the owner chooses to deny it. He can say, 'That's not my dog,' and there is nothing the RSPCA or anyone else can do about it.

We should think also of the consequences of allowing dogs to roam the streets. I have already shown the costs incurred when dogs run loose and are involved in accidents or cause injury to people: £77 million a year.

Then there is the question of police time and how it is used. Anyone would be rightly angry if a friend or relative was robbed or raped, and later discovered that a policeman had been nearby and could have helped them – but he was chasing a stray dog at the time and was not free to do so.

In the House of Commons, MPs recently voted that dog registration was not necessary. However, when the Bill reached the House of Lords it was thrown back. I believe that the Lords were much more in touch with the wishes of the people and, as an unelected body, were able to vote according to their conscience. The MPs, on the other hand, the elected body, voted along party lines and not according to how they personally felt about the issue.

As a nation, moreover, we are out of line. Only weeks after the Commons vote, in November 1990, the European Parliament voted overwhelmingly in favour of dog registration. This was in response to a motion brought by the British MEP Anita Pollack. Its purpose was to introduce an initiative that would help to restrict the spread of rabies and place pet dogs in a more secure environment. At present in the EC, the UK, Belgium and Luxembourg are the only member states to have made no provision for dog registration.

I am disappointed in the attitude of the Kennel Club, who also maintain that a registration scheme is unnecessary, yet they carry out more registrations of pedigree puppies and dogs per year than any other organisation. Unfortunately they are only interested in pedigree dogs. I think they should have the welfare of all dogs at heart. At the very least, were a registration scheme to be introduced, they could offer to regulate their own members. Better still, they could act as consultants in designing a new scheme that covers all dogs.

Registration may sound bureaucratic and expensive, but it need not be. Other forms of registration have long been part of daily life. Cars are registered, and so are televisions. When you go to buy or rent a television set, the sales assistant warns you that you need a licence for it. The licensing authority is automatically notified that you now have the set, and you face a large fine if you do not buy a licence to go with it.

It is obviously not beyond our powers to work out and operate a dog registration scheme on similar lines. The dog and the owner would then appear on a national record. If the dog went to a new owner, this fact would have to be communicated to those running the registration scheme, as is the case with motor vehicles. If the dog became dangerous, and had an order against it stating that it had to be kept under control, this too would go on its record.

The existence of records would also make it possible, say in the event of an accident, for there to be some comeback against the owner.

In time, every dog in the country would be registered, and would have to wear an identity tag. That is the ideal solution. If an owner failed to register a dog, or allowed it to stray, he would be in trouble. If he denied ownership, there would need to be some means of proving that he had control over the animals or was responsible for it. If he wanted to keep it, but failed to register it, he would risk having to give up the dog, which eventually would be removed from him.

If any dog was found straying, it would be taken in by the dog warden – and there should be many more dog wardens than there are at present to enforce this practice. Then, if the owner could not be found, and no-one else offered to give it a home, it would be put down.

Such rules may sound cruel, but in no more than the short term. Already we put down 90,000 dogs a year, and that is far too many. In the long term a system on those lines would save a great deal of suffering.

As to the precise form a registration scheme would take, there are many possibilities, and these will need careful consideration and discussion. It is fairly clear, though, that dog owners will have to pay something. A charge will be needed to cover the administration of the scheme, the cost of employing dog wardens and so on. How much it should cost is another matter. I think the scheme would need to be flexible. There could be a tiered system, for example, under which a social group such as the elderly would be exempt; the charge for a spayed bitch or a neutered dog might be less than for an untreated animal, and there could be other exemptions and reductions.

I am quite sure that a fair and workable system can be devised. As I have said, if we can do it for material things such as cars and televisions, there is no reason not to extend the principle to dogs.

Finally, to anyone who still says we cannot afford such a scheme, I say we are already paying out £77 million a year to cover the cost of stray dogs and the damage they cause. That is the negative way to do things. The positive way is to set up a registration scheme and banish stray dogs from our streets.

MY CHARTER FOR ANIMALS

In the previous chapters I have covered a lot of ground and now want to summarise what has been said. As I hope you will agree, we have a very long way to go in Britain before we can truly call ourselves a nation of animal lovers. Below I have set out my own provisional Charter for Animals. From dogs to circuses, it sums up the wrongs we still commit, or allow others to commit, and in each category proposes an action plan.

ALL OWNERS OF ANIMALS
Certificate of Competence
I propose that future animal owners should have to obtain a certificate showing that they are capable of taking on the responsibilities of ownership and are thoroughly conversant with those responsibilities.

This is the kind of idea that is greeted with scorn by politicians. 'Can't be done' is their usual response. 'Too expensive to run. Impossible.' That is nonsense. At the RSPCA in Leeds we ran successful courses in animal first aid. As an Animal Care Tutor with 'Y' Training, which is the training agency run by the National Council of YMCAs, I now teach young people who go on to gain employment in the field of animal care. This two-year course covers many aspects of animal care and could be adapted and introduced into schools at primary level. The curriculum should include first aid for animals, grooming, diet, housing and so on. Evening courses could be organised for adults who wish to own pets. Specialist organisations such as the British Horse Society already run diploma courses relevant to specific animals.

Age limit on ownership
At present the lower age limit for buying a pet from a pet shop is 12 years. This should be raised and limited to young people who are earning money and able to provide for all the animal's needs, including veterinary fees.

DOGS
Undoubtedly the animal that suffers most in this country is the one we call our best friend, the dog.

Pet dogs
Pet dogs are frequently ill-treated, starved, or deprived of proper veterinary treatment. They are dumped on motorways, and abandoned when owners move house, go on holiday, or find that the novelty of keeping a dog has worn off. They are left to roam the streets, where they form packs as they would if left to live wild. They run into parks and school playgrounds, frightening people and sometimes attacking them.

Action plan
- Require all dog owners to obtain a Certificate of Competence, showing they understand the responsibilities of owning a dog and are competent to care for it.
- Set up a National Dog Registration scheme. This would record the name and current address of the dog's present owner, and must be up-dated in the case of any subsequent owners. To help identify dogs, a micro-chip to be inserted under the skin.
- Set up compulsory license scheme for dealers and pet shops.
- Ensure that all breeders are licensed irrespective of the number of animals kept for breeding. There should be a mandatory Certificate of Competence in Canine Husbandry, and regular

inspections of premises. Introduce the registration of stud dogs for breeding as well as bitches.
- Ban puppy farms. There are far too many dogs in existence for the number of homes available.
- Stop the transit of unaccompanied puppies over long distances by road and rail.
- Impose automatic fines on anyone allowing a dog to stray without reasonable excuse.

Guard dogs

Dogs are acquired, sometimes through theft, to be sold abroad as guard dogs. They endure long distressing journeys and rarely survive longer than six months in the hot countries they are sent to, such as Nigeria. In the UK, guard dogs are left for many hours without company and are encouraged to be vicious.

Action plan
- Ban the export of guard dogs.
- Require guard dogs in the UK to be kept under the supervision of a handler at all times.
- Institute regular inspection of premises using guard dogs.
- Ensure that *all* sections of the Guard Dogs Act 1975 are enforced – not just some, as at present.

Fighting dogs

Dog-fighting exploits the loyalty of a dog towards its master, and causes death and horrific injuries.

Action plan
- Those found guilty of organising, or conspiring to organise, a dog fight should face an automatic prison sentence.
- Dog-fight organisers already face being banned from keeping a dog. Extend this to conspirators.
- Dog-fighting magazines and videos should be declared obscene and illegal. Their publishers should face an automatic prison sentence.

CATS

Cats enjoy nothing like the protection given to dogs, however inadequate that may be. As they are not licensed, the law does not require any notification of any accident that involves cats. Yet cats are classed as property. They are stolen from their homes by gangs trading in their skins. They also fall foul of those people who set traps and snares.

Action plan
- Require cat owners to obtain a Certificate of Competence.
- Encourage owners to join cat clubs. Grooming for shows teaches good husbandry and promotes health.
- Track down and punish cat thieves.
- Ban the use of traps and snares.

BADGERS
Although it is illegal to dig for and bait badgers, these brutal activities are widely practised.

Action plan
- Enforce the relevant legislation (Badgers Act 1973, Wildlife and Countryside Acts 1981) efficiently. A Government Inspectorate would have the necessary staff to investigate and prevent crimes against these animals.
- Introduce automatic prison sentences for offenders, together with hefty fines and confiscation of equipment used on digs, including vehicles.
- Impose an automatic ban on keeping a dog, if the dog is used for digging badgers out.

COCK-FIGHTING AND QUAIL-FIGHTING
These medieval sports are illegal but continue at underground venues.

Action plan
- Introduce prison sentences and heavy fines for those found guilty of pitting birds against each other.
- Ban the practice of keeping quail in bags for long periods of time. Make it an offence to transport any bird in this manner.

HORSES AND PONIES

Television has glamorised showjumping and eventing, and more and more children want to own a horse or pony. Meanwhile the overbreeding of stock has brought down prices, and these animals are now too easy to buy. Owners buy with nowhere to keep the horse, then tether it out on spare land where it is neglected. Rag and bone men force horses to pull carts that are unroadworthy and keep tack that is not in good condition or is ill-fitting.

Action plan
- Require prospective owners to obtain a Certificate of Competence.
- Require prospective owners to provide proof that they have adequate facilities for housing the animal.
- Ban whips altogether for young riders. Organisers of equestrian events should discourage the use of the whip at all levels.
- Ban the practice of tethering and make it illegal to turn a horse, pony or donkey into a field with no adequate shelter.
- Ensure that all horse-drawn carts display the name and address of their owner.
- Require all tack to be in a good state of repair and fitting properly according to precisely defined codes.

WILD BIRDS

Although the RSPB is an active champion of birds in Britain, more care is needed for the common everyday species – starlings, blackbirds, sparrows, magpies and so on.

Some licensed keepers hold birds in their care for longer than is necessary. Birds are wild creatures and should be returned to their natural way of life, not kept as exhibition pieces.

Action plan
- Institute more education in schools to teach respect for birds in the wild.
- Ban the use of air rifles, other than in organised rifle clubs.
- Plant more hedgerows and trees in our countryside and towns to encourage a healthier stock of birds and other wild animals.

WILD ANIMALS

The legal status of wild animals in this country varies from species to species. Some, like the grey squirrel, are classed as vermin. Others, like the red squirrel and badger, are afforded considerable legal protection. In my opinion all wild animals deserve some protection.

Action plan
- Introduce clearer, more wide-ranging legislation to protect wild animals and to replace the current inconsistent laws.
- Ban the use of snares, traps and other pieces of equipment which cause needless pain to wild animals (and domestic animals too).
- Institute an educational programme for schools on the rights of wild animals, so that young people grow up respecting wild animals.

ANIMALS IN TRANSIT

Animals suffer needless discomfort on journeys by road or sea to slaughterhouses which are long distances from the markets at which they were sold. Legislation intended to set minimum standards for animal welfare on such journeys is inadequate.

Action plan
- Introduce legislation compelling purchasers to have animals slaughtered at the slaughterhouse or abattoir nearest to the point of sale.
- Encourage meat dealers to export frozen carcasses by banning the export of live animals and introducing appropriate incentives.

FARM ANIMALS

Most farmers care about their animals, although some care more about cashing in on subsidies. The laws covering farm livestock are numerous and complex.

Action plan
- Remove responsibility for farm animals from the Ministry of Agriculture, Food and Fisheries and include it in a Ministry

for Animals which would have an Animal Inspectorate to carry out frequent unannounced inspections.
- Revise the laws to produce an agricultural package that every farmer can understand.

ZOOS

There is no doubt in my mind that zoos are a thing of the past and should be phased out. Animals do not belong behind bars.

Action plan
- Encourage zoos to close and convert the land to other leisure uses.
- Stop the breeding of animals that cannot be returned to the wild.
- Arrange funding to care for current zoo animals until the end of their days.

CIRCUSES

I can see no justification whatsoever for circuses which use animals. The life of these animals is miserable, worse than that of zoo animals which at least have a permanent home. Circus animals must spend many days of the year on the road, moving from place to place in cramped, distressing conditions.

Action plan
- Encourage circuses to close or continue without animals.
- Arrange funding to care for current circus animals until the end of their days.

EXPERIMENTS ON ANIMALS

Animals have suffered greatly through unnecessary experiments in laboratories: forced to inhale tobacco, injected with untried drugs, their eyes, coats and skins treated with experimental substances, and so on.

Action plan
- Examine the need for any further experiments using animals.
- Work towards a total ban on the use of animals in laboratory experiments.

EDUCATION

Finally, I want much more attention paid to educating people about animals. We should now be thinking about teaching Animal Care in our schools as a normal part of the curriculum.

If we had a national Animal Inspectorate, as outlined in this book, its existence would liberate the private animal societies and charities from the duties of seeking to enforce current legislation. They could then do so much more in the important fields of preventing cruelty and running education programmes for the public at every age level.

WHAT YOU CAN DO

The very fact that you have given your time (for which I thank you) to read this book says to me that you have an interest in the wellbeing of animals.

But just to read about animals is not enough. What can you do to help?

HELP BY EXAMPLE

Perhaps the most important way to help is for you to take a look at how you yourself behave towards animals and the habitat in which they live.

Listed below are some points that just might help you avoid causing suffering to animals.

THE PROPER CARE OF WILD BIRDS

Wild birds are very different from the captive birds that people keep in the home. They are very largely self-sufficient and should be left alone to sort out their lives, except in an obvious emergency.

People interfere too much. Wild birds fall into human hands for all kinds of reasons, and one of our worst failings is to charge in to help when it is not needed. We have this unfortunate talent for 'finding' wild birds before they are lost.

When fledglings (the feathered young) come out of the nest, not all of them are strong enough to fly and some end up on the ground. When this happens, the mother will come and feed the bird on the ground until it can fly off and look after itself. Remember, the reason it is on the ground is that it is trying to *leave* the nest and become independent.

So if you find a fledgling on the ground, the first thing to do is nothing at all. Don't pick it up, just leave it there. If you want to, move back a few yards and keep a watch on it for a few minutes from a secluded position. Sooner or later, in most cases, you will hear it calling to its parents, and like as not the parents will answer. If this happens, all is well and there is no need to do anything. (If the young bird is unfeathered and clearly has fallen out of the nest by accident, you can try to locate the nest and put it back. This is only for pre-fledglings.)

If no parent comes, go away and come back two hours later. If the fledgling is still there, don't rush in. Wait. The bird may well be in contact with its parents – only you were not there when it happened.

Carry on watching. Wait until you are quite sure the fledgling is not being fed, maybe for another hour or so. Then, and not before, you can step in and try to help.

It is not easy to raise a young bird. Most people fail. There is no way that we can regurgitate food like the bird's mother. Nature has its own systems and they are difficult to emulate.

If a bird, of whatever age, has an obvious injury and is in distress, that is a genuine emergency. If it seems to have fractured a wing or leg, try to capture it and take it to a vet for treatment. The best way to capture it is to throw a towel over it and transfer it to a suitably sized box. Hold the wings close to the body to prevent further injury. Any bird that is not diseased will resist capture: if you can pick up a bird that has no obvious injury, it may be too ill already and may not recover; but you can still try to save it by taking it to a vet.

After an accident or a close encounter with a cat, the bird may suffer shock. Here you can help by placing it in a dark, well-ventilated box. Leave the box in a warm, quiet room and give the bird at least one hour to recover. As soon as the bird seems ready, try to release it to its own environment. Do not try to keep it. That is an offence.

Most larger birds will present more problems than a non-expert can cope with. A swan tangled in fishing tackle, for instance, or an oiled seabird, requires careful handling by a trained person. In such cases, contact your local branch of the RSPCA (you will find the number in the phone book).

As a general rule, it is better to seek expert advice for all injured birds. At the back of your mind you may remember having read a children's adventure story in which the young hero or heroine saved an injured bird by putting its leg in splints made from matchsticks. In some versions the bird is a racing pigeon, and next day takes part in a 1,000-mile race which it wins easily. There was a time when stories like that were popular and widely read. Such stories should never go beyond teaching young readers to be generally kind to animals. They should not try and turn them into amateur vets. Before anyone starts thinking about attempting to heal an injured bird, he should consider also that a botched effort may cause further injury and unnecessary suffering to the bird.

My advice is to seek the help of a vet – and hope he will offer free treatment. In my view, you should not have to pay for a vet to examine and deal with a wild bird. The bird is part of nature and as such, belonging to no-one, is no one individual's financial responsibility, so I believe that a vet should give his services for nothing. This does not always happen. Some vets charge private individuals and charities such as the RSPCA, regardless of whether the animal is wild or not.

I have heard of vets charging £50 or £60 for treating an injured seagull. To me this is wrong. A veterinary surgeon should *want* to treat the bird free of charge. Vets make enough money out of treating our pets and farm animals, and I think they should make a general exception for wild life.

THE AVOIDANCE OF DANGEROUS LITTER

There are other ways to help wild animals, and birds in particular. Accident prevention is one of the most important, and here I would like to make a special plea to fishermen, who fish for pleasure beside our rivers and canals.

Despite countless warnings and noticeboards on the bankside, fishermen are sometimes very untidy people. They leave hooks lying around, for example, and throw away masses of household rubbish which they should be taking home with them.

Their carelessness can be particularly hazardous to swans. It is a natural habit of swans to look for food by sieving in the water with their bill. Recently I went to help an swan with a hook deeply embedded in its bill. It took a long time to get it out. To make matters worse, the poor swan had taken down a great length of fishing line which we had to ease gently out of its digestive system.

It was a young bird, still to shed some of its immature brown plumage, and it was very distressed by our arrival on the scene – as were its parents which were swimming nearby. We had to get hold of the young swan and lift it off the water before we could remove the hook and the line, and then we took it away to a vet for a checkup and a dose of antibiotics. This disturbed its parents even more, and when we brought the young bird back, they went frantic with delight to see it again.

This whole episode could have been avoided if the fisherman had cleared up after him and had taken his rubbish away. It is no good for these people to complain, as they sometimes do, that no litter bins were provided. I know there are not enough bins beside our rivers and canals, but some fishing waters are so remote that it would be impractical to leave a bin there. No-one would empty it, except vandals who might well throw the contents in the river.

The real responsibility is always with fishermen, and I wish more of them would recognise this. Angling societies could help by fining members who leave litter on the banks. I know some which do this, and some which also threaten members with expulsion. I welcome this initiative, and ask them to keep up the pressure.

For their benefit, and for others who use our woodlands and fields for walks and picnics, let me outline some of the other problems which arise from dangerous litter:

- **Ring-pulls from cans**. Larger birds can choke on these, or swallow them and damage their intestines. Small birds push their beak through the hole and the ring-pull is fixed around the beak.
- **Plastic can-pack holders**. Birds get tangled in these. In their efforts to free themselves, they panic and pull the plastic mesh tighter round their legs and body.
- **Crisp packets**. Birds peck at the packet, tear off a strip and try to swallow it.
- **Wire**. Any piece of loose wire left lying around is dangerous to birds, for obvious reasons. Workers laying cable or repairing fences should be careful to remove any remnants when they leave the site.
- **Glass**. Again it is obvious that glass fragments can cause cuts, and damage birds which try to swallow them.

Many of these dangers apply as much to young children as they do to birds and other animals. For all their sakes, please pick up and remove any dangerous litter you may come across – even if it is not yours – and take it home with you.

HELPING OWNERS IN DIFFICULTIES

If, by the way, you know an elderly or disabled person who is worried about the fate of his or her pet should they *suddenly* have to go into hospital, you can get them a useful card from the RSPCA. There is one which states: 'In the event of an emergency please ensure that my pet (name) is cared for (address).' Another card says: 'In the event of an emergency please contact (name and address) who will care for my pet.' On the back, the owner fills in the details of the pet, the owner's name and address.

Like donor's cards, people should carry the appropriate pet card in their bag or wallet whenever they go out. Then, if there is an emergency, say they collapse or are involved in an accident, the local authority or the independent helper can be notified.

YOU AND THE LAW

Most police forces have Wildlife and Countryside Liaison Officers. It is to these officers you should go with information relating to badger-baiting or anything that relates to the criminal mistreatment of wildlife including people taking birds from the wild. These officers are also well informed as regards dog-fighting. They can be contacted at your local police station in person or by phone. While most people contact the RSPCA to report acts of cruelty, it is perfectly correct to report these matters to the police. After all, these acts are covered by criminal law.

MAKE OTHERS AWARE

When you are trying to change the attitude of people towards animals, the most important thing is to make yourself heard. Why not join or even start up a pressure group? If running a group is not quite your scene, then why not join one of the animal welfare societies already in existence. There are many of these that cater for all kinds of animal interests.

CONTACT CENTRAL GOVERNMENT

Politicians are there to serve you and they want your vote. So let them know that you care about the conditions animals live in.

Tell them, for example, that you want the export of live animals for meat to be stopped now. At the time of writing, I have just learned that the total number of animals exported live for slaughter in 1991 was 1,186,402, a 43 per cent rise on the previous year. These figures included a dramatic rise, 60 per cent, in the number of sheep sent on these long distressing journeys of death, 488,909 in 1990 to 773,502 in 1991.

If you feel as strongly as I do, make your voice heard. Write to your MP and demand the banning of this terrible trade in animals. The more letters they get, the more notice MPs will take. Ask them if they care about animals. Tell them that you will no longer support needless experiments on animals.

Tell them that you require a Minister for Animals with a properly trained Inspectorate to deal with all issues that concern the welfare and rights of animals, including the power to punish those who commit wrongs against animals.

CONTACT LOCAL GOVERNMENT

The same goes for local councillors. Make them ensure that zoos, boarding, breeding and riding establishments, together with pet shops in the council's area, are all properly licensed and run.

Ask them if they are aware that premises such as this are in need of regular inspection by trained officers who are fully conversant with the needs of animals.

Tell them, too, that we need a Minister for Animals with a properly trained Inspectorate to carry out these duties.

Tell them they need your vote. Make them earn it.

CASEBOOK

DOG-FIGHTING:
THE HALIFAX CONSPIRATORS

To break into the illegal ring of the dog-fighters, we badly needed information. Like every RSPCA Inspector, I had my sources – a colleague who had spotted an interesting chain of events; a journalist; an advertisement in a newspaper; a contact on the fringe who wanted to talk, but whose tip-offs were of variable quality and were sometimes even deliberate misinformation.

My colleagues and I spent hours, many of them in our off-duty periods, waiting about in likely places, not knowing whether our quarry had decided to abandon his plans at the last moment or shift the venue. The dog-fighters' circle was proving difficult to penetrate. They were well organised, operating with the stealth of criminals, surfacing briefly and then vanishing for weeks and months. Some indeed had criminal records. Many had the inherent weaknesses arising from a violent nature. Someone, sooner or later, would open a door for us. We had to be patient.

Meanwhile, the life of an RSPCA Inspector was never quiet. All kinds of calls came in day and night, concerning kittens abandoned in a box; someone starving his dog; a farmer neglecting to bury dead livestock and so on. Our working lives were crammed with emergencies, and the pile of paper in the in-tray was always as high as a block of flats.

I knew that pit bull breeders were organising dog-fights in my immediate area of West Yorkshire, but so far our leads had not produced the clinching evidence we needed for a prosecution. Then, on 20 January 1988, I received a phone call at my office in Leeds that caused me to drop everything I was doing.

With a colleague I drove to Bradford Central Police Station. There we met a Detective Constable of the Major Crime Support Unit. He had a sheet of paper that he wanted to show us. While searching a house in Halifax he had come across the document, photocopied it and returned the original.

He passed the paper across. One look was enough. This was hot, definitely the best piece of evidence we had seen in months. It was a crudely hand-printed contract between two men, witnessed by a third, to fight two dogs at an undisclosed venue at 10 am on Sunday 20 March – exactly two months ahead.

There was little doubt in our minds that the document was genuine. It was headed 'Pit Bull Contest, Contract'. It gave the date and the purse – '£200 each'. The fight was to be 'under Cajun Rules', and a match report was to be sent to *Pit Bull News*. There were three signatures: P. Ford and M. Symons, who were described as the owners, and F. Rogers, who had witnessed the contract.

The police officer went on to explain that Ford – in whose house he had found the contract – was certainly involved in some way with pit bull terriers. On the day of his search he had found four dogs kennelled at the house, and so when he came across the contract he felt more than confident that an organised fight was planned.

That day I drove back to Leeds with feelings close to elation and a headful of possibilities. Back in my office I laid the contract on my desk and started to work out precisely what we had in our hands.

We had just entered ourselves in a race. We had two months, or sixty days, to find out where this 'private venue' was, stake out the place, raid it when the fight was under way, and make our arrests. If everything fell into place, we could throw the book at them – the owners and anyone else present. A successful court case would also be one in the eye for *Pit Bull News*, which was clearly implicated in the fight. This would make nonsense of its crass, hypocritical claim, printed on the first page of every issue: '*Pit Bull News* does not in any way endorse the use of Pit Bulls for illegal purposes.'

The time element was in our favour, I reckoned. But if we could not catch the organisers red-handed, it would be just another near-miss and nothing worthwhile would be achieved. The law, as ever, offered us little flexibility.

As for our suspects, we had located one man and one address: Peter Ford, aged 36, and living in Halifax, known to keep pit bull terriers at his house. Further inquiries were to reveal that Ford worked as a night club barman-cum-bouncer and had a long criminal record. We also found that one of the dogs matched the description of 'Brutus, a red dog', named in the Contract.

We had two other names to work with – M. Symons and F. Rogers. In my RSPCA group I had four inspectors, located in Bradford, Skipton, Huddersfield and Halifax. I circulated copies of the contract to them and next day Derek Woodfield, our Halifax man, came to see me.

He brought with him a Statement of Person Under Caution.

He had taken it some two years before while investigating the ill-treatment of a dog. It was signed 'F. Rogers'. As Derek and I compared the signatures, I saw him smile. I nodded my agreement. There was no doubt that the signatures were by the same hand, the hand of Frederick Rogers, a shop owner from Halifax.

Then came our first setback. We checked out the shop that Rogers had been running, but he had sold the business and moved on. We decided to stick to the task of tracking him down and two days later we had our reward. Rogers was living in a street not far away, in a house which backed on to a disused railway line.

That was two out of three. We had no direct lead to Symons, the owner of the other dog, but knowing from his record that Ford had connections in the Durham area, I spread the net further north. I talked to my RSPCA colleague in Durham, who turned out to be very well informed about pit bull owners living on his patch. He thought the name Symons was familiar and I went up to Durham to see him. In the course of my visit he showed me plenty of houses which had pit bull terriers living in sheds in the backyard, but alas, when we found his Mr Symons, he was not the right man.

Back in Leeds, I studied the fight contract for further clues. No luck there. We would have to concentrate on the two men we had, Ford and Rogers, watching their homes and following their movements up to the morning of the fight.

It would not be easy for our small group to handle the surveillance of two houses and two men coming and going from them. I contacted RSPCA headquarters in Horsham and asked if their Special Investigation Unit could be assigned to the job, but they were not available.

I reviewed our position. Quite apart from the manpower shortage, there were other obvious shortcomings. To start with, our blue or white Ford Escort vans would give us no cover at all. The rotating air vent in the roof stood out like a beacon and was impossible to conceal even when the van was parked among other vehicles. A small conversion job was called for. Suddenly Derek Woodfield's van took on the insignia of a non-existent firm called 'Fir Tree Securities'.

We could get round the van problem by using private cars as much as possible, but that was not ideal because our radio equipment was in the official-issue vehicles. What was more, both houses would be difficult to survey without alerting the suspects or some nosy neighbour.

Ford's house was especially tricky. The street he lived in was one of a series of parallel side roads running into a main road. Ford lived in a terrace of back-to-back houses with little to distinguish one from another, although his house did have a dormer window with a stone facing which would help observers during their watch periods.

Our options were also severely limited by a row of bollards, intended to prevent through-traffic, which cut the street in half. If we parked in the fairly short run of street which contained Ford's house, someone would be sure to spot two men sitting inside a car for long periods of time. Local children in this area are not slow to come forward with their usual difficult questions – 'What are you doing?' or 'Are you the police?' – and relaying the answers to their parents and others. In the end we chose to observe the house from a side road on the other side of the main road, almost in line with the street where Ford lived. The angle was tight, but we could still see far enough into the street opposite to get a view of Ford's house.

One thing was in our favour. We knew that Ford worked at a night club in the town centre, and we soon established that he did not seem to take any of his dogs to work with him, so we could probably get away with just watching the house during his non-working hours.

The street where Rogers lived offered various vantage points. It is a long busy road and we could probably hide away successfully either in front of the garage quite near the house or in a pub car park on the far side of some open ground. We also noted with some satisfaction that there was a public toilet conveniently located nearby. (They make these stake-outs a lot more comfortable, believe me!)

Neither position gave us a complete view because Rogers's

house was set back from the street on a service road. Our best place to park, we decided after further debate, was a third point from where we could clearly see the gate leading to both the front door and the side door of the house. Rogers parked his vehicle, a white van, on the service road outside this gate.

In the weeks that followed, we watched each house as often as we could manage. Meanwhile our routine daily work had to go on and many sleepless nights lay in store, particularly for Derek Woodfield and myself.

Our first priority was to get a general picture of life at the two houses, to see who came and went, and when. In addition, I needed more inside information about the dog-fighting world. If we could penetrate the ring at some other point, we might be able to glean valuable knowledge that would lead us back to Ford and Rogers. Our case would surely stick better if we could establish connections between our two suspects and the network which appeared to involve many of the readers of *Pit Bull News.*

Our manpower problem remained acute. If anything, it grew worse as we became increasingly tired. Then, by a stroke of good fortune, I received an approach from an old friend and some-time working partner.

Bruce Smith, a reporter with the *Yorkshire Evening Post*, for which I write a weekly column, had covered many local animal stories for the paper, and I remembered several occasions when he had not been afraid to take his coat off and help me. The protracted and tragic case of Knaresborough Zoo was a prime example. When the zoo's organisation collapsed, and I suddenly found myself struggling to care for 300 neglected animals, Bruce's practical and generous help had been invaluable.

Bruce had become alert to the news potential of dog-fighting. He had noticed the growing number of advertisements appearing in Yorkshire newspapers for pit bull terriers. He asked me if I knew any of the breeders who were selling these dogs, as he had it in mind to investigate the pit bull market, to see what the buyers and sellers were up to and to what extent they were involved in so-called 'sporting' activities.

I decided to take Bruce into my confidence. I told him about the contract we had discovered and described our work in the last few days. I took him over to Halifax and showed him the houses we were keeping under observation.

He was immediately keen to help, and offered his own services as an observer. We could also use his car, he said. No-one would recognise it.

All right, I told him. That sounded fine. Another pair of eyes would be a great help. I had no doubts about Bruce. He had already proved his value as an ally. Now I was wondering if I could push my friend a little further.

My problem was, I still lacked a proper 'in' to the dog-fighting fraternity. There were various ways of doing this. One was to go to a weightpull competition. This is the respectable front of the dog-fighters, where dogs are harnessed to heavy flat-bed trolleys loaded with weights, and must pull the trolley as fast as possible over a short course.

For such events the dog-fighters could hire a legitimate hall, and provided everyone stayed within the rules of the competition there was nothing the RSPCA or the police could do to prevent them. I had found out that a weightpull contest was due to be staged shortly near Liverpool.

I put this to Bruce as a possibility. I could not possibly go myself, I said. After the *Animal Squad* series of programmes on television my face was too familiar. In fact, you could reckon that any RSPCA Inspector would be known to the underworld figures living within his patch. We needed an outsider.

There was something else, I said. We could help ourselves a lot if we could register a dog with the legitimate Pit Bull News Gamedog Registry. I already had some copies of *Pit Bull News*, but membership would ensure a regular supply and would almost certainly lead us to further useful information.

Bruce agreed to report back to his editor and see what he could arrange. The meeting was positive. The *Yorkshire Evening Post* would fund the buying and registration of a pit bull terrier. Bruce would be responsible for finding a breeder and doing the deal. We also contacted the Leeds RSPCA Animal Home Kennels and they offered to pay for any vets' fees and the cost of boarding the dog.

At this stage Bruce introduced a colleague, Richard Taylor, who joined the investigation team. He was to play a full part in the coming weeks and became an important partner.

Together we immersed ourselves in the murky lore of dog-fighting. A recent successful raid on a barn close to Potters Bar, near London, had yielded precious evidence, including a video of a fight.

We studied advertisements for pit bull puppies, and selected a breeder in Bradford who boasted that all his dogs were 'from very game bloodlines'.

Bruce now went underground. He became Bob Cutts, pit bull enthusiast, with an accommodation address to cover his tracks. He and Richard telephoned the breeder and fixed a time to visit his kennels.

They drove to a council estate not far away. The breeder opened the door to them. He wore a Leeds United lapel badge and his living room was a minor museum to his two obsessions. Leeds United mementos and slogans covered the walls, and soon he was pulling out photograph albums of what he said were champion dogs in both Britain and America. Some of the photographs showed dogs training on treadmills.

The man was confident and persuasive. The dog he had for sale was called Max, a red and white male. He was asking £150 for him. He produced a pedigree going back four generations and explained that Max had been sired by Jasper, which he co-owned. Jasper was a one-time winner, he said later, and had featured in a video seriously damaging the leg of an opponent. (This match, we later found, was reported in *Pit Bull News*.)

'My dogs are special,' said the breeder, 'whatever you want them for.'

He fetched the puppy, and to the consternation of Bruce and Richard he was a poor-looking specimen, undersized and unhealthy. Bruce told him that Max did not look up to much, and he agreed to drop his price to £125. 'The others in the litter each fetched more than £300,' he said. 'But this one had an early illness. That's why he's small.'

Bruce said he would take the dog, and asked about training him. The breeder said Max could go on a treadmill when he was about ten months old. He said he could supply them with a treadmill but they were expensive, about £200 to £250 each. Or they could get an electric treadmill for between £350 and £450.

Bruce and Richard took the puppy back to Leeds. He obviously had a rupture and was in poor general health. He was examined by a vet. Her report clearly showed that the dog had been badly cared for.

The vet estimated Max's age as 11 weeks. He weighed $4^{1}/_{2}$ lb, which is underweight for a dog of his age and size. He had an undershot jaw and was suffering from an umbilical hernia. He had mild mange, and both eyes were extremely sore and watery from conjunctivitis, which required treatment. The vet went on:

'His main problem was his general bodily condition which was very poor. He had obviously been reared on an unbalanced, inadequate diet resulting in early rickets which had caused deformity of all legs but which was affecting mainly the carpal and stifle joints.

'His general behaviour was also strange. Although he could walk, albeit with a strange gait due to his crooked legs, he was reluctant to do so and spent his time lying down. He appeared unused to moving around and was liable to cringe at any sudden movement by any human around him. I believe that it is probable that he spent his life confined to a small box or cage and was not used to running around. This would also be hindering the normal development of his joints and bones and adding to his already poor conformation which was resulting from the rickets.'

Readers may think that, for £125, we had bought ourselves the proverbial pup. Perhaps we had, but I was glad that the poor animal had been rescued. He was now in good hands and his condition quickly improved. Today he enjoys a life of freedom on an estate in Scotland, with no worries about what his next opponent will do to him.

Armed with Max's pedigree certificate, Bruce Smith (alias Bob Cutts) sent off £3 to the editor of *Pit Bull News*, who placed the dog on the Gamedog Registry and told our Mr Cutts that he could now order *Pit Bull News* direct from him at £12 per year.

We continued our surveillance of the two houses in Halifax. Even from a distance, the features of the principal inhabitants were becoming familiar. Ford looked tough and fit when seen in daylight, and wore a moustache. At other times he was a shadowy figure walking to and from his bouncer's job.

Rogers was bulky, low-browed and belligerent-looking, and

sported a crew-cut. We rarely saw Mrs Rogers, but we felt it was unimportant. Very few women are players on the dog-fighting scene.

On 13 March the British Pit Bull Association held its winter show at the Aughton Show Centre, a grandiose name for a converted farm building near Ormskirk. Originally the show, a legitimate event, was to have been held at the Wythenshawe Forum in Manchester, but protests by residents led the local council to ban pit bull events on City Council property.

So on that Sunday morning a crowd of some 400 people arrived in Aughton, paying £2 a head to enter the show organised. Among them were Bruce Smith and Richard Taylor.

They took secret photographs and later, when the Ford-Rogers fight date had passed, they published an article about the show in the *Yorkshire Evening Post*. They wrote about the main attraction, the weightpull competition, and were even more impressed by the macho behaviour of the crowd:

'Heavily tattooed dog-owners with skinhead hair cuts and ear-rings strutted about the hall with their powerful and aggressive pit bull and Staffordshire terriers ...

'Throughout the day owners allowed their fearsome dogs – strapped in spiked harnesses – to snarl and confront each other only inches apart ...

'On prominent display was an oil painting of Jasper, the fighting dog which sired Max, the dog bought by the *YEP*.'

They noted that many spectators ignored the show ring in favour of private talks conducted in huddles around the hall. They overheard guarded talk of fighting, 'rolls' and treadmill training.

For many the highlight of the day was a fight which broke out between two spectators. Unable to cope with their own tensions and the threatening atmosphere in the hall, fuelled by the relentless barking and snarling of the dogs, they started shouting insults and then went for each other. They were pulled apart, then went outside the hall to carry on their fight. Many bored spectators followed, but the scrap was soon over. Obviously, neither man was as brave as he expected his dogs to be.

When Bruce told me about their day at Aughton, it sounded a thoroughly nasty occasion. But then, given some of the people present, how could it have been anything else?

It was less than seven days to the dog-fight. We stepped up our observations, borrowing cars from colleagues and friends and keeping our issue vehicles well away from the target houses. This gave us a communications headache because our radios would always be in the wrong place, as I have already mentioned. There was nothing for it; we had to get by as best we could.

We were joined by RSPCA Inspector Barry Fryer. He had dealt with dog-fights before and his advice was shrewd and generously given. He also made his private car available, which was not only a useful addition but a very fast one too.

The manager and staff of the Halifax Animal Home made a room available to us for making hot drinks. Here anyone off-watch could grab an hour's sleep and a wash before returning to their watching post.

I had also made contact with the local police station, dealing with a Chief Inspector. I put him fully in the picture and he in turn promised to lay on the necessary police presence on the morning of the fight.

The intervening days vanished at speed and, on the Saturday evening before Sunday 20 March, I went to a meeting at Halifax Police Station which had been set up by the Chief Inspector. Also present were two very experienced senior detectives, a Detective Inspector and a Superintendent. The Superintendent, as things turned out, was to make the most telling contribution of all.

The plan we agreed was simple enough. My colleagues and I would keep up our observations through the night. Next morning, teams of police officers would join us in raiding the two houses and make any arrests that were necessary.

There were several loose ends. We still had no further information on the man Symons. If he really was the owner of one of the dogs, he might arrive at one of the two houses shortly before the fight, presumably with his dog. On the other hand, he might not. It all depended on where the 'private venue', mentioned in the contract, was actually located. Right now, with only hours to go, we still did not know.

Rogers, as witness to the contract, might have a further role to play in the fight. On the other hand, he might not. We just did not know. However, we had done some discreet snooping and we knew that he kept pit bull terriers and had some form of pit in the rear garden of his house. Although it was very unlikely that he would risk using it for a full-blown fight, it might be used to test two dogs out. It was still worth sticking close to Rogers, wherever he went in the next few hours.

Even more seemed to depend on the movements of Ford. He owned one of the dogs, called Brutus, and would have to take it to the fight. If the fight was at his house – and we knew that he had a cellar large enough to stage one in – he would stay at home on Sunday morning. If the fight was to be elsewhere, we had to hope that he would lead us to it.

It was particularly odd about Symons, I thought. How was it that no trace of him had surfaced in any of our investigations?

Before the meeting ended, I broached another, related idea that had been on my mind since the beginning of the case. It was simply this: supposing there was no fight at the appointed time. What then?

'We have a contract,' I reminded everyone, 'but we have no idea where the fight is due to take place. At present, all we can do is to make sure we know exactly where Ford and Rogers are at all times between now and ten o'clock tomorrow. Just doing that won't be easy, but that must be our objective, no matter where they go.

'But,' I concluded, 'what are we going to do if there is no fight?'

The Superintendent looked pensive for a few moments. He had only recently seen a copy of the fight contract for the first time. When he did speak it was in a calm and commanding voice that held the attention of all present.

'Well,' he said, 'If we cannot find them fighting the dogs, it seems to me that there is here a case of conspiracy to fight.'

In one sentence he had gone to the very core of our dilemma. The remedy he proposed was brilliantly simple. Even though it had never been tested in court, it gave me enormous heart to think that there could be a way forward should we not be able to catch the dog-fighters red-handed.

I left the meeting at Halifax Police Station a much happier man, promising to return for a final briefing at 06.30 the following morning. I went back to my team and told them about the chances of securing a conspiracy charge. They too were delighted by this development. The no-fight situation was something we had discussed in the past, but this was the first time any of us had received such promising support from the police. Everyone was very tired but morale was high, and my latest news undoubtedly gave them an extra lift that would help them over the next difficult hours.

For my part I had had very little sleep for the last seven days, and just hoped I could keep my concentration through this final stretch of the stakeout. I was grateful to have Inspector Barry Fryer with me as an adviser. He did a lot to make sure the decisions I took were the right ones.

Together we discussed each situation as it arose, and he quietly offered his previous experience with dog-fighters and what they were likely to do. He did this in a way that never challenged my position as officer in charge, and to this day I remain grateful to him for his understanding and help.

That last evening was not without its lighter moments. Around nine o'clock I received word that Ford had left his house and was heading, without dogs, towards the night club where he worked. I went down to the club to join Bruce Smith and Richard Taylor who were keeping watch on the entrance from Richard's car.

'Is he in there yet?' I wanted to know as I climbed into the back seat.

'Not yet,' said Bruce. 'We haven't seen him yet.'

I pulled a face. By my estimation Ford should have arrived by now and therefore the two newspapermen should have spotted him. It was too important to leave to chance. If Ford had gone off somewhere else, we needed to know this as soon as possible, to give ourselves the best opportunity of tracking him down before ten o'clock next morning.

I suggested to Richard that he go into the club and have a drink, look around and make sure that our man was in there. If he was, then we could all relax for a while. This would also allow some of the others to stand down and have a rest. It might be the last chance they would get before morning for a quick spell of shut-eye and a wash and brush-up.

Richard agreed and got out of the car. Quite a stream of people had been entering the club while we sat in the car, and now Richard followed them and disappeared inside.

Ten minutes later he came out. He turned away from where we were parked, walked round the block and rejoined us in the car.

He sat down, looking thoughtful. He did not speak, just sat there.

'Well,' I said, when I'd had enough of his silence, 'is he in there?'

Richard nodded – to the great relief of Bruce and myself – and then went back to his silent pondering. I thought he seemed embarrassed about something.

'Well, come on,' I said. 'Tell us what's going on in there.'

Eventually, he did. The first part had been easy, he said. He bought a drink, and saw Ford doing his job as usual. He finished his drink and then went to the Gents.

Wrong move? At first he could not tell. It was like a dream, full of unexpected turns. A man going for a pee walks in through a door marked 'Gents'.

The small square space which opens before his eyes is filled, to his astonishment, with a sea of bulging white thighs belonging to figures wearing corsets, black stockings and garter belts. Reflected in the mirror, he saw a bare arm applying dark red lipstick to a jowly face topped with bushy dark eyebrows. Another figure had a fishnetted leg hooked up on the wash basin and was doing something distinctly personal with a razor.

Richard blenched before this tableau of harpies. His eyes swung back to the sign on the door. Was this the Ladies? No, it wasn't. It was the Gents. *And these were blokes*! The realisation hit him, his eyes rounded in horror, and he immediately did what any respectable journalist would do. He shut the door and got out fast.

Bruce and I smiled quietly to ourselves. 'Oh,' I said after a while, 'it's that sort of a place, is it?'

'I don't know,' said Richard. 'It must be.' Then he added, 'I didn't even get my pee.'

A few minutes later, the mysteries of transsexual Halifax came out of the closet. A gathering crowd of men and women emerged from the club and other parts of town, all clad in basques and other skimpy lingerie. They strutted and hobbled on high-heeled shoes past our car, heading for a late performance at the local cinema. The *Rocky Horror Picture Show* was on that night and its fans were out in force to celebrate its rituals of throwing rice and dressing in outrageous costumes.

In the car Bruce and I chuckled away at Richard and his predicament in the Gents. In the end Richard also got round to seeing the funny side. Then we settled down to a long watch until the club closed and Ford went home.

Once he had left work and was safely indoors, we drove to Rogers's house. Observers there reported a number of comings and goings during the day. Rogers himself was at home. In the early hours of the morning a couple of visitors called, one of them arriving in a pickup vehicle and spending some time at the back of the house. The porch light was left on all night; usually it was turned off. Mrs Rogers had returned home very late.

I finished my evening's observations and with Bruce and Richard ate a watery curry in an insanitary Indian restaurant. Then I went back to the Halifax Animal Home to rest for a couple of hours. I finished the night folded up once more in the cramping confines of our observation car. We had less than seven hours to go.

Before dawn on that Sunday morning I went to Halifax Police Station for our 06.30 meeting. Teams of police officers filed into the room and the briefing followed. It was professional and to the point. RSPCA officers were allocated to the police teams, and groups were assigned to cover the houses of Ford and Rogers. It was agreed that if no further suspicious movements took place, visits would be made to both houses.

I teamed up with two detectives in a police car. We took up a position near Rogers's house and, with the other teams deployed at strategic points, settled to wait for the ten o'clock deadline, ready to act if either of our suspects made a move before that time.

The minutes went by slowly, turning into hours. Each house had a visitor, but no dogs were seen. A feeling of grim disappointment began to come over me. After two months' unremitting work, nights without proper rest and all the attendant discomforts – terrible food taken on the run (last night's curry was still gurgling revenge somewhere in my tubes) and no chance to relax or read a newspaper without the fear of missing a vital clue ... After all that, were we to end up with nothing? As ten o'clock came and passed, it began to look like it.

I sat on with one of the detectives. 'Just give it a few more minutes,' we agreed. But what then? As 10.30 approached, we knew we must act. At last we radioed the orders. I drew a deep breath and opened the car door. We were going in.

I crossed the familiar no man's land to Rogers's house, which was called 'Oakwood', and knocked on the side door. Rogers opened the door. We introduced ourselves and told him what we were there for. Rogers was cautioned and was told him he was being arrested. We then entered the house.

I went into the living room. A bull terrier bitch came up to us. Fortunately she was friendly. I looked at the walls, lined with framed certificates of pit bull terriers and their pedigrees. Copies of *Pit Bull News* lay on a table with posters headed 'Oakwood', offering treadmills and pups for sale at £650 each. The poster thanked a certain 'P. Ford' for 'the use of Brutus'. This was one of the first pieces of evidence linking Rogers with Ford. Another leaflet declared:

'Oakwood Bonzo is a very game 1 time winner. He is black and weighs in at 40lb fit'.

In the absence of a fight – and there was no sign of any disturbance in this house – all these pieces of evidence were essential if we were going to make a conspiracy charge stand up in court.

Police officers began to seize some of the documents. They found a series of photographs showing dogs working a treadmill. The dogs, we later established, were owned by Ford and Rogers.

In the cellar I found a workshop used for turning out breaking-sticks. A number of sticks lay about in various stages of manufacture. The finished ones were painted with the word 'Oakwood'.

In the garden Rogers had a shed with a dog run. Inside was a black male pit bull terrier. This was my first meeting with Bonzo. He was a well-muscled dog but he had a lot wrong with him. His legs were badly scarred and he appeared to have a problem with his left eye, which also had a scar on it. There were scars on his left shoulder and both ears were badly mutilated. I gave the order for the dog to be taken away and in due course my colleague Derek Woodfield came and collected him.

Nearby in the garden was a treadmill in working order, and the fenced enclosure we already knew about, which could have been used as a practice pit to give dogs a 'roll', a sort of trial fight or sparring match.

The police took Rogers away to Halifax Police Station. Back in the house, I turned the pages of *Pit Bull News*. Suddenly a name leapt off the page at me – 'Oakwood'. It stood at the bottom of a poem that had been reproduced. The gist of the poem, the name of the dog and the name 'Oakwood' all pointed to this being Rogers's work.

At Ford's house the team leaders were a police Sergeant and RSPCA Inspector Barry Fryer. Ford was cautioned and told he was being arrested. He had four dogs with him that morning. In the ground-floor living room were two which he said were Brutus and Honey. In the basement he had two more, called Joker and Dirk.

Barry's experienced eyes ran over Brutus's body. The dog had scarring around the face, muzzle and front legs. Hours later, a vet examined Brutus and reported that the scarring was from bite marks caused from five to seven days previously.

As yet we had no clear evidence of a fight, but the net seemed to be closing around Ford. In the living room Barry also found a leather pulling harness.

They went down to the basement, which was divided into two cellars. The larger measured about 16 feet by 14 feet and had a stone floor partly covered with sawdust and wood shavings. There were several piles of dog excrement and both cellars smelt stale and unpleasant.

On one side of the cellar was a wooden kennel occupied by a young female pit bull terrier. This was Joker and she appeared to be in good condition. On the floor by the kennel was an old motorcycle tyre. 'It's used for training,' Ford told them.

Shelving covered the entrance to the smaller cellar. There they found Dirk, a red brindle and white pit bull terrier, chained to another kennel. He was lean and well-muscled, but had a lot of old scars and several recent wounds. His left ear was badly torn, and he had fresh injuries to the chest, the lower lip and jaw. Blood could be seen on the wounds. The dog's eyelids were very swollen and causing irritation to the eyes which had yellow matter in and around them.

This dog and Brutus were taken away and the vet, after examining Dirk, said that all his injuries were caused by bites. He thought the fresh wounds were three to four days old.

The other principal find at Ford's house was a set of six hardwood panelled doors, such as dog-fighters use to make a ring.

Had there been a fight? It certainly looked as though Brutus and

Dirk had been in the wars, even if the fight had taken place several days earlier.

One of the first things to do in any case involving cruelty to an animal is to establish ownership. Later that day, Ford admitted that he owned the dog Brutus. Dirk, he claimed, was not his. He said he was looking after him for a friend who was serving a prison sentence.

When pressed, he admitted that he had care and control of Dirk, and had looked after him for the last four months. The police questioned him about the dog's injuries, and he said:

'It had some, obviously it's been used for fighting and badger-baiting and things. But it was all healed.'

He was asked about Dirk's fresh injuries. He claimed that Dirk and Brutus had got together by accident:

'Yes. Last week Brutus got at Dirk and they were bang at it.'

Had he taken Dirk to a vet for treatment?

'No. I didn't think it was serious.'

This was a considerable step forward. Although we might not be able to prove that the Brutus-Dirk encounter had been the organised dog-fight described in the contract, the evidence of the recent injuries to the two dogs clearly indicated that Ford, at least, was accustomed to inciting pit bull terriers to fight.

As for Rogers's involvement, there was no doubt that he owned Bonzo, but Bonzo was not mentioned in the contract. To link Rogers and Ford, we had to rely on the other evidence of the photographs taken from Rogers's house, one of which showed Ford holding Bonzo. Under questioning, Rogers later admitted that he knew Ford and said that the treadmill in his garden in fact belonged to Ford.

It seemed as though we had enough to bring the case. As a result of the evidence gathered, both Rogers and Ford were charged and bailed.

A further break occurred the following day when the third man, Symons, came to light, uncovered after some rapid work by the police. Symons did not in fact live up in the Durham area, but right here in Halifax. When brought in for questioning, he admitted that he had been present when the contract was drawn up and that he, Ford and Rogers had signed it. He explained that he did not own a pit bull terrier but had been trying to buy one. Perhaps this explained why the name of his dog had been left blank on the contract.

Like Ford and Rogers before him, his get-out line was that the contract was not genuine but a 'fantasy' or a 'joke'. At the time I felt this would be a weak excuse to offer in the face of a conspiracy charge. Ultimately, however, that was for the courts to decide.

It was now a matter of putting together all the evidence, and gathering the many statements of those involved in the case. For me it meant checking through notes that had been accumulating since first meeting at Bradford Central Police Station, all of two months ago.

Legally, the case was now in the hands of the police. In due course, all three men appeared at the Magistrates' Court in Halifax to answer a charge of 'Conspiracy to commit the summary offence of causing, procuring or assisting dog-fighting'.

After various appearances at the Magistrates' Court the case was sent to the Crown Court in Leeds. The decision to prosecute was taken by the Crown Prosecution Service a month later.

It was to be nearly a year before the case came up before a jury at Leeds Crown Court. This was particularly hard on the three dogs that were taken into care. Brutus and Dirk were not improved by having to live in kennels in the close company of strange dogs. The confinement excited them and made them even more dangerous and difficult to handle. They bit their handlers and were forever trying to jump walls and get among the other dogs. After a while we began to doubt whether it would ever be possible to release them to ordinary life with new owners.

As the law stands, we had no choice but to detain the dogs until the case against their owners was resolved. I do not so much quarrel with that as with the enormous time-lapse between the initial charges being brought and the case coming to court.

The fate of Bonzo was even worse. He too was a difficult dog to look after and had to be moved to various places. Eventually he was taken to kennels at Bawtry, near Doncaster. Despite our efforts at security, word of his whereabouts reached the dog-fighters. A gang broke into the kennels, cut the wire of the cage and stole the dog. Later, I heard, Bonzo was put back to further slavery on the fighting circuit.

Ford, Symons and Rogers each had their own barrister and the first day of the hearing was entirely taken up with claims that the case was wrongly brought. The defence counsels well knew that this was the first case of its kind ever to be brought and were determined to try and throttle it at birth. The judge ruled that he was convinced that the case should be heard.

They also objected to the veterinary surgeons and me being called as expert witnesses. The judge ruled that this could be challenged when we appeared in the witness box. Finally the jury was sworn, the defendants pleaded not guilty and the trial was adjourned to the following day.

That evening brought a nightmare for me which lasted until next morning. My weekly column for the *Yorkshire Evening Post* appears each Monday. Weeks before, I had written a standby piece about dog-fighting, and that day the sub-editor had picked it up, thought it was topical and put it in the paper. The article focused on New York and the reaction of the city authorities there to a recent spate of deaths and injuries to humans caused by American pit bull terriers.

I had not sought to hide my views about dog-fighting, but fortunately the article contained no direct references to the present court case. As soon as I saw a copy of the paper that night, my blood ran cold. This could be big trouble.

Next morning all three defence counsellors came into court brandishing copies of my article and asked the judge to throw out the case. To my great relief the judge ruled that I was entitled to my opinion, even though I had been perhaps unwise to express it at such a time. After further entreaties from the defence he ruled that the trial should go ahead. It was certainly a lesson in tactics for me that I shall not forget.

I do not propose to describe the events of the case in detail, since much of the time was taken up by the usual technical sparring that you get in any court case. However, one or two incidents are worth recalling in view of the historic nature of this trial.

One concerned the evidence of the Detective Constable who started the whole investigation when he found the fight contract in Ford's house. The defence argued that he was in the house on other business and had no right to steal the contract. The detective stood his ground. He had not stolen it, he said. He had taken it, photocopied it, and had put it back.

If the defence had broken through at this point, our case might have been wrecked, but the judge decided that he had acted while in the course of his duties and had not done so improperly.

I was next to give evidence. The defence challenged the fact that I was being put forward as an expert witness. The jury was sent out while this point was settled. I was asked if I had ever taken part in a dog-fight. I replied no, but I had studied videos.

I was asked if I considered myself an expert on dog-fighting. I replied that only those who took part in fighting regularly and handled the dogs that fought, could claim to be experts. That was something I did not wish to do.

The judge asked what I knew about dogs that were used for fighting. I told him that I had studied the subject by reading books and case files, and by watching videos and talking to people who had been involved in it. I told the court something of what I had learned about the history of dog-fighting since the eighteenth century and about the types of dog taking part. I was not, I said, an expert in dog-fighting, but as an Inspector of the RSPCA I was a trained person who had expertise in dealing with people who broke the law appertaining to animals.

The judge told the counsels that he was more than convinced that the prosecution had brought a witness who could be called an expert. There was a further objection from the defence which the judge overruled. This was important, both for the present, first-ever conspiracy case and all future cases, because it established that an RSPCA Inspector could be regarded as an expert witness.

The jury was recalled. I was cross-examined, fairly gently, and several police officers were called before the court adjourned.

The following day came the first breakthrough, when Rogers changed his plea to guilty. The judge asked the members of the jury to return a verdict on Rogers and they declared him guilty by a unanimous verdict. He was to be sentenced later.

The fourth day of the trial was mainly taken up with the defence. The jury retired and came back the same day to announce guilty verdicts on Ford and Symons. Next day the judge sentenced Ford to five months imprisonment, Symons to three months and Rogers to one month.

It had been a long and difficult case, but we had won and made history. The charge of 'Conspiracy to cause, procure or assist at dog-fighting' is now case law. I hope it will be used again, in fact as often as it needs to be until we have eradicated this barbaric activity from society.

Readers may feel that the prison sentences were not long enough to be effective. I would only say that it is still a considerable achievement in animal welfare cases to procure any kind of prison sentence. Since the trial, moreover, maximum fines for attending dog-fights have been increased from £50 to £1,000, while sentences for organising a fight have been increased to six months imprisonment and fines increased to £2,000.

Thanks to the Case of the Halifax Conspirators, we have travelled forwards. There is a lot to do, as I have already said, to educate children, youths and adults away from even thinking that we have the right to make any dog fight and inflict terrible injuries on another dog. We shall not have won this campaign until the disgust felt towards dog-fighting is universal.

BADGER DIGGERS
IN HUMBERSIDE

One dark winter's day shortly after Christmas, three men set off from Leeds on a badger-digging expedition. They drove north-east in the direction of Bridlington on the Humberside coast taking with them two tan terriers and a black 'roughcut' terrier, a trained and battle-scarred working dog said to be worth £450.

About halfway between York and the coast, they stopped the car. Not far from the road was a copse. The men got out of the car, collected their dogs, a pair of spades and a supply of canvas sacks, and headed for the copse.

The farmer, who owned the copse, was out on his land when he spotted the men. Knowing that it was a badger wood, he had no trouble in guessing what they had come for. Rather than confront them, he withdrew quietly to his farmhouse and phoned the police.

When finally the police raided the copse, the dig was well advanced but not going at all the way the Leeds men had hoped. Two dogs had been put underground. There they met with fierce resistance from the badger, to the dismay of the diggers who were huddled by the entrance. The police ordered the men to get the dogs out of the sett. While this was going on, they looked around for evidence of what the men had been doing and noticed the crudely piled earth from fresh diggings near the opening to the sett, and the sacks and spades lying nearby.

The two dogs, when recovered, were in a sorry state. When my RSPCA colleague in Humberside examined them, he had no doubt that they had been in head-to-head confrontation with an animal or more than one animal, and that the fight had been underground.

One terrier had been savaged about the mouth. The left side of its face was soaked in blood, it was bruised, exhausted, muddy and in a state of shock. Giving evidence in court, the local vet said that both dogs also bore scars from previous wounds.

The black 'roughcut' dog had terrible bites on the right side of its face. When it came to the surface, blood was oozing from its mouth and it had cuts to the inside of its upper lip.

The three men were arrested. Two were charged with digging for a badger, attempting to take a badger, and causing unnecessary suffering to a dog. The third was charged with the two badger offences.

The accused pleaded not guilty to all charges. True to form, they advanced the old and tried excuse that they were not looking for badgers at all. They had set off from Leeds to hunt for rabbits and foxes in the Bridlington area, they claimed. They took a wrong turning on the road and ended up near the copse.

While sorting out their route they noticed rabbits running in the road. They left their car and gave chase. Moments later, two of the dogs ran into the copse and dived down a hole. To their surprise they realised it was a badger sett, and they were waiting for the dogs to come out of the sett when the police arrived.

The story counted for little with the Magistrates. All three accused were found guilty on all charges. Two were sentenced to two months imprisonment for causing unnecessary suffering to their dogs, banned from keeping a dog for four years and fined £250 on each of the badger charges. The third was similarly fined on the badger charges.

The case went to appeal, where the judge reduced the prison sentences to one month each but told the two men, 'These charges are so serious that you must go to prison.' He also reduced the fines facing all three men but refused to reduce the four-year bans on keeping a dog. 'That is not a day too long,' was his verdict.

Photographs of the two dogs, taken by the police, more than adequately bear out the judge's view. To me it is quite abhorrent that men should subject their dogs to such a terrifying and painful ordeal. Sport has nothing to do with what these dogs suffered.

BESSIE: A VICTIM OF
DOMESTIC VIOLENCE

THERE is a pretty little village in Dyfed, West Wales. It stands about a dozen miles from the coast.

For some years in the 1970s I was based in Aberystwyth and the village came within my territory. I made inspections at the weekly cattle markets in the nearby towns, and at the occasional Saturday horse sales. While in the area I used to visit this village and call on an RSPCA member who lived there.

The population was curiously mixed. About two hundred original locals lived in and around the village, their numbers declining slowly in tune with the general drift of younger people away from their country roots and into the towns. Then, in a series of waves, small tribes of hippies moved in. The newcomers set up communes in the area, and took over cottages and farmhouses as they fell vacant.

The locals eyed these representatives of the new or alternative culture with suspicion. In their reactionary way they resented the freedom enjoyed in the communes. They disliked the newcomers' folk and rock music, their bright clothes, and, especially, the fact that they did nothing all day *and* received state benefit for doing so. To the average original local, the hippies were 'parasites', members of a disreputable underclass. That they should get away with what they did was 'a national disgrace'.

One of the many things that niggled the locals was the way the hippies treated their animals. No-one from the city could possibly know how to keep hens and goats, or so the locals thought. Therefore, it followed naturally, they must be maltreating them. So, from time to time, I received complaints about so-and-so and their animal: 'It's half-starved, I've seen it', or 'It can't walk, they leave it tied out all the time.'

Whenever I went to investigate these complaints, I was welcomed in the communes and left free to check on any animal I liked. Not once did I come upon a case of cruelty. The impression I formed was that these people valued their animals highly, and were prepared to go without themselves rather than let their livestock be deprived.

To find cruelty, I went instead to the local cattle markets and horse sales. There some of the local farmers freely demonstrated their indifference to the welfare of animals. They took calves to market stuffed in the boots of their cars. I saw sheep being unloaded from the backs of vans. The animals had not been properly restrained and could well have injured themselves, either against the sides of the vehicle during the bumpy road to market or against some object left on the floor of the van, such as a spare tyre or some tool with a metal edge.

On a summer's evening Janet Morgan was listening to records in the front room of her cottage. Above the sounds of the record she began to hear another sound. It was a kind of scream. She turned down the volume on the record-player and listened. The screaming continued, high-pitched and intense. She thought at first it was the sound of two dogs fighting, but then she realised it was something very different. It was the desperate noise of one animal screaming in pain.

Janet knew that the people in the large house opposite her cottage kept a dog, a spaniel. She had heard the dog whining on previous occasions, but tonight the sound was different. It was definitely the sound of a dog in extreme pain. What could be happening?

She turned off the record-player and went over to the front door. She opened it and stepped outside on to the road. She noticed that the gates to Hillview, as the house opposite was called, were closed, and the house was in darkness. The screaming had stopped now, but the more she looked at the house the more certain she was that the noise had come from somewhere within its walls.

Whatever the disturbance had been, it now seemed to be over. Janet listened for a few seconds longer, then went back into her cottage. She put on the record-player again.

Further up the main road which runs through the village, on the opposite side from Janet's cottage lived Rebecca Smythe. She had just put her children to bed and was standing by the window of the front bedroom.

It was a warm evening and the window was open. Through it came a persistent sound which she later described as a 'whining'. She thought it was probably the whining of a dog. But it was an unusual sort of whine, she noticed, one that built up into a scream of pain. It occurred to her that it was more like the sound of an animal that was being hurt *at that moment*, rather than the sound it would have made in, say, the aftermath of an accident.

'The screams really frightened me,' she told me later. 'They went on for such a long time. I felt that I ought to go out and investigate, but I couldn't leave the house because of the children.'

She also said that she thought the sounds were coming from the direction of Hillview. Like Janet Morgan, she remembered that the time must have been close to 8.30 pm, as she always put her children to bed at that hour.

Three people lived at Hillview: Mr and Mrs Harry Jones and their son Bryn. The son, aged 24, worked as the manager of a shop in a nearby village.

For some time the relationship between father and son had been strained. The father, aged 69, was acknowledged to be a difficult man to live with. He wished to be thought of as deeply religious, said the son later, but his beliefs seemed to weigh heavily on him. Of all the days of the week, he was at his most irritable on Sunday. He forbade the use of gas and electricity in his own house, and no food could be cooked. But, as Bryn well knew, while he and his mother went without, the head of the family went off to visit friends and ate heartily with them.

On Tuesday 8 August, Bryn and his father had more than their usual disagreement. Bitter words were spoken, and these had led to a long argument. The already sour atmosphere between the two men grew openly dangerous. Bryn decided it would be wise to leave the house for a while, to cool off and let things settle.

He called Bessie, his 10-month-old liver and white springer spaniel, and together they set off for a walk in the hills close to the village.

As they walked, Bryn reviewed the grim position that he and his father had reached. It was one of those long-running family rows that never seemed to get anywhere. Bryn felt there was no way he could back off, he had to go on sticking up for himself. And his father, so far as he could see, showed no sign of relenting in his view of how his son should behave. They were at a point of stalemate. Up there on the hillside, Bryn decided it would be best for them all if he went away for a couple of days. He needed to get out. He was afraid of what might happen if the arguments grew any fiercer. It would do his mother good, too, to have a break from the bitterness and discord.

Bryn returned to the house at around 11.00 pm. He had a brief talk with his mother, who agreed to feed the dog while he was away, then he placed Bessie in the outside toilet in the yard and left her there. He climbed into his car and drove out of the village. He did not return to the house until late the following evening, about 10.00 pm.

We now move to the morning of Thursday 10 August, the day after Janet Morgan and Rebecca Smythe had heard an animal screaming from, they thought, the direction of Hillview.

Derek Rees, a welder by trade who lived in the village, was walking down the road when he was approached by Mrs Jones, Bryn's mother, whom he knew quite well. Later he told me:

'She stopped me as I was walking along. She looked distressed about something, deeply worried. She asked me if I had a moment to spare.'

Mrs Jones then asked him if he would come with her into the yard at Hillview. It was very muddy in there, she warned him, so he went home first to fetch his wellington boots.

He rejoined Mrs Jones and they walked through into the yard and approached one of the outhouses. As they went towards the buildings, Mrs Jones said, in a shaking voice:

'Harry killed Bessie last night.'

She pointed to the open doors of the garage. Rees noticed some tools just inside the garage. The tools were spattered with blood. There was blood on the garage doors, and Mrs Jones pointed out a smear of blood on the floor of the garage. It was streaked as though someone had quickly swept a brush through it.

They went further into the garage. On a bench at the back Rees found a hammer. Its head was covered in blood. He showed it to the white-faced Mrs Jones, who nodded and led him back outside to the yard. She stopped in front of the outside toilet. She said nothing, but pointed at the door.

Rees opened the door. What he saw made him physically sick. He stepped back quickly into the yard, doubled over and vomited. Lying towards the back of the toilet was the body of Bessie, horribly disfigured. Her battered head was covered in blood, and a large pool of blood lay on the floor.

When Rees had recovered a little, the two went into the house and stood in the kitchen. Feelings of anger and revulsion flooded through Derek Rees, a quiet man who cared a great deal for animals. Mrs Jones had distressed her friend, but, as events were later to show, she had chosen a good ally.

'I felt sick,' he later told the court. 'I felt I had to do something about it and the only thing I could think to do was to contact the local RSPCA officer - and this I did.'

Rees made the call to my office from Hillview. I was out at the time, and he had to leave a message on the answering machine. When I returned, not long after, I listened to the tape and then drove out to the village as soon as I could, and reached the house at 2.10 that afternoon. On the way I stopped for a brief word with the local policeman, who knew the Jones family well.

Harry Jones was at home at the time of my visit. I introduced myself to him and told him why I had come. I asked him if I could see the springer spaniel that was kept on the premises.

He showed me into the yard. We walked across it to the outside toilet. He opened the door and there I was confronted with the sight that had made Rees so violently ill. Bessie lay in her own excrement, a mass of blood around her head.

It was too dark and cramped in the toilet to examine the dog's injuries, so Jones went in and pulled the body out into the yard. Now, as I looked more closely, I could see there were a number of wounds on the head. One in particular was very deep. When I moved the dog, dark blood flowed out from this wound.

From my position, crouched on the floor, I looked across to where Jones stood. He was wearing wellington boots, and the left toe had a dark stain on it, like blood which had dried.

I asked Jones if the dog belonged to him.

'No, it's my son's,' he replied.

I asked him if he knew what had happened to the dog.

'No,' he said.

I straightened up and looked around the yard. On the ground was a trail of bloodstains leading to the garage. The doors of the garage were open and inside I saw a number of tools on the floor. All of them bore bloodstains.

The trail continued across the floor of the garage to a work bench in the right-hand corner. The floor had been roughly swept and bloodstained shavings lay in a pile in one corner.

On the bench was a vice, and alongside the vice lay a hammer. Its head had blood on it. There were also some hairs sticking to the hammerhead. I could not be certain, but they seemed to be the same type and colour as Bessie's.

I asked Jones if he could account for the blood and hair on the hammer.

'Duw,' he replied, 'I knocked a nail in the wall with that hammer this morning. I didn't notice anything.'

We went back into the yard. A car was parked there. The rear offside door had blood marks on it.

I went indoors to speak to Mrs Jones. I asked her when she had last seen Bessie alive. She replied that she had fed and watered the dog at 7.30 the previous evening, then she took it out and shut it up in the outside toilet.

She added that her husband had come home that evening in a foul mood and had made angry remarks about Bessie. Then he had ordered his wife out of the house. She could go and see Miss Williams in the village, he said. He wanted to be left at home by himself.

Mrs Jones went out at 7.45 pm, she said. The car was parked in the yard when she left. She came back at 9.50 pm to find no-one at home. About ten minutes later her son came in, having spent the previous night away. Mrs Jones recalled telling him he should go straight up to his room to avoid meeting his father who might come in at any minute.

Her husband arrived back at about 11.00 pm, she told me. That was all she was prepared to say about events that evening.

I felt I needed to record the scene as it was at that moment. I arranged for photographs to be taken, also for a piece of hair to be taken from the dog so it could be compared with the hair on the hammerhead.

I told Jones that I also wanted to take his left wellington boot away, to see if the blood on it matched that of the dog. A post-mortem would be carried out on the dog, I advised him, and if he wished he could nominate a veterinary surgeon to be present. He declined this offer.

Jones was then cautioned in English and Welsh and I took a short statement from him. (Today the procedure is slightly different. Governed by the Police and Criminal Evidence Act of 1984, it requires that interviews must be recorded 'contemporaneously'. Each question and answer is written down at the time of the interview, and afterwards the interviewee is asked to sign each of his answers.)

Later that day I returned to Hillview and interviewed Bryn Jones, the son and owner of the dog. Although clearly upset, he was not afraid to speak frankly. During the interview the father continually interrupted, complaining that I was forcing his son to tell lies about him. I pointed out to Mr Jones that his son was 24 years of age and more than able to speak for himself.

When that interview was finished, I took the body of the dog away and drove it to a vet who carried out his examination. In his report he later told the court that death had taken place at some time during the previous 36 hours. He went on to say:

'The head was covered with clotted blood which had come from a depressed skull fracture which amounted to a jagged edged hole about two inches in diameter in the centre of the skull. Small fragments of bone had chipped off and were embedded in the underlying brain substance.

'The upper lip and tongue were wedged firmly in the closed jaws indicating a position of excruciating agony at the time of death.

'Haemorrhage must have been extensive as it had left the muscles and internal organs virtually void of blood. The muscles and subcutaneous tissues of the head were bogged down with bloodstained fluid.'

He described the other injuries he found on the dog and stated that, in his view, 'The head bruising, and nature and extent of the bone and brain damage, indicated that it had been caused by a blunt instrument rather than a pointed surface, whose surface area was probably under 2 inches in diameter.'

In concluding his evidence, the vet said of the wounds that 'their nature and position were the result of repeated blows, rather than one impact as might be expected from, say, a road traffic accident.' Ten days later, on the afternoon of Thursday 17 August, I made a return visit to Hillview. I had received the results of the post-mortem and also had confirmation that the blood on the wellington boot and the hair on the hammer both matched the samples taken from Bessie.

I had also interviewed various neighbours, including Janet Morgan and Rebecca Smythe, and so had been able to pinpoint when and where the killing had taken place. Both women told me it must have been around 8.30 pm when they heard the animal screaming. Both also indicated the direction from which the sound had come. I then drew a map of the village street, marking their respective houses and Hillview. When I drew lines from the women's houses pointing towards the direction of the screaming, the lines crossed in the yard of Hillview.

It seemed clear enough to me that, in a fit of uncontrollable rage, the father had killed his son's dog. Getting him to admit this would be another matter.

Harry Jones seemed to live in an increasingly bitter and shrinking world of his own. His relationships with his wife and son could hardly have been worse. Now he had tried to assert his authority over his son by committing a messy and brutal act of cruelty. The fact that the killer had made so little effort to conceal either the blood or the murder weapon pointed again to the father. It was *his* hammer that had been used to kill the dog, and blood from the dog had been found on *his* wellington boot. These two pieces of evidence appeared to implicate just one man in the killing – Harry Jones.

When I arrived at the house, Mrs Jones was at home but her husband was out. I said I wanted to take a statement from her, and this we did. Shortly afterwards, around 3.00 pm, Harry Jones came home. I told him I had some further questions to put to him and reminded him that he was still under caution.

I asked him about the blood on the head of the hammer. 'Whose was it?' I wanted to know.

'The dog's,' he replied without hesitation. 'It went in there after the accident.'

This was a new development. No-one had mentioned any accident until now. If Jones was going to claim the dog had got out and been injured in the road by a passing car, this did not tally with the vet's report. The vet had confidently ruled out a traffic accident, stating that death had been caused by blows to the head made with a blunt instrument.

I decided to pass over the 'accident theory' for the time being.

'There was a dog's hair on the head of the hammer,' I went on, 'and it had blood stuck to it. What was this hair doing on the hammer?'

'I don't know about that,' was Jones's reply. 'Perhaps the dog was lying down there for a while.'

I asked Jones to explain how the dried blood had got on his wellington boot.

'You should know the answer to that,' he retorted. 'It was when I carried the dog out of the toilet so you could see its head. It must have touched my boot.'

I pointed out that this was not correct as the blood on his boot was already dry before he touched the dog.

He began to falter. I pressed home my questioning. 'Blood doesn't dry that quick, does it?' I said to him.

His answer produced another sign that he was beginning to feel annoyed and frustrated:

'Well, Duw! Duw! You won't prove it!'

After a pause I said, 'Where were you on the night of 9th August, Mr Jones?'

He thought for a moment and replied, 'Fishing all day from two o'clock until seven, then I came home. I stayed in until eight-thirty, then about that time I went up the pub. I came home about ten o'clock.'

I then pressed him to agree that no-one else except him had been in the garage. He assented, and also agreed that the dog had been killed with a hammer. He said he was the last to use the hammer – to put a nail in the wall:

'I saw blood on the hammer but not the hair,' he said.

I pushed on with my questioning. 'You know the dog was killed with your hammer in the garage ...'

Here he suddenly interrupted. 'No, no,' he replied. 'I'll never believe that. The dog was seen injured on the road outside.'

'Who saw the dog on the road?' I asked him.

'I'm not going to mention his name now,' he replied.

It was clear that Jones was having difficulty in holding his story together. He was trapping himself in a web of his own making.

Next, I put it to him directly that he was the one who killed the dog. I asked him when he had last seen it alive.

He replied, 'At eight o'clock in the yard.'

I tried again. 'What I am saying is that because the garage is yours, and the hammer is yours, and there was dried blood on your wellington boot – and because you have agreed there is no possibility that any other person would do such a thing to the dog in your garage ...'

Again he interrupted me. 'I have been breeding dogs for ten years,' he began suddenly. 'I told him to get rid of her and change her for a labrador. They can be better trained for the gun.'

Again he had introduced a new topic. Significantly, this was the first time he had admitted falling out with his son over the dog. I already knew from his son that he and his father had argued over Bessie, but this was the first mention he had made of the subject to me. Jones was becoming more and more agitated. I carried on with my line of questioning.

'Your son was away at the time. So was your wife. You were the only one at home ...'

He must have felt I was getting too close, and broke in again:

'How do you know what time the dog was killed?' he said. 'You have no proof – only what those hippies have said.' He quickly added, 'They said I reported them to the Social Security.'

I waited for a moment. This was yet another strange intervention. I had certainly not given him any hint of what the two women, Mrs Morgan and Mrs Smythe, had told me about the timing of the dog's death. And here was Jones trying to smear their credibility as witnesses. They say that in small villages everyone knows everyone else's business. Even so, this sounded to me like a rather desperate assumption.

I continued by saying that I felt he was not telling me the truth. His neighbours could in fact verify the time of the dog's killing – and all the evidence pointed at him.

'They're only hippies,' he said with a sneer. 'There's no proof. No-one will believe them.'

How wrong Jones was. The court did believe them, and rightly so. The case came up before the magistrates on 8 November. Jones was accused of the following charge:

'That he did on the 9th of August....cause unnecessary suffering to a certain animal, namely a dog, by unreasonably killing it in an improper manner. Contrary to Section 1 Sub-Section 1(a) of the Protection of Animals Act 1911, as amended by the Criminal Law Act 1977.'

After a hearing which lasted nearly two days, he was found guilty and fined a sum of £80 and ordered to pay costs of £100; he was given six months to pay.

As I watched him walk away from the court after receiving his sentence, I reflected on what a strange case it had been. An elderly man, until then a respected member of the community in his village, had been exposed on the evidence of witnesses he despised. His family life had been laid bare in the most painful way, and all his frailties of character had become public knowledge.

None of this would help the dog, of course. It never did. Bessie was gone, and perhaps only Bryn Jones and his mother would mourn her death.

Incidents such as this make me think a great deal about the value we place on our family pets, and in darker moments I wonder why some people keep them at all.

NEEDLESS SUFFERING

Mrs Ballinger was a difficult woman. Aged 51, she lived in a run-down district of Leeds with two adult sons, both of whom had prison records, and a young daughter aged nine. She was hard of hearing, had a vicious temper and lived in a state of undeclared war with her neighbours. During my inquiries I sought help from several people living nearby who refused to co-operate. Mrs Ballinger had already been after them, shouting threats at anyone she thought might speak against her. In that neighbourhood there were many who preferred a quiet life, and that was all they were prepared to tell me.

I first called at her house with a colleague, following up a report that she had a sick dog and had not been caring for it. From the start we had problems with her hearing.

To make myself understood I had to resort to a mixture of shouting and writing down questions in my notebook, then holding the notebook up for her to read.

Eventually she admitted that she had a dog. She went indoors and fetched a brown and white puppy which she held up to us. The puppy was in good condition.

'Do you have another dog?' I wanted to know.

'No', she said, 'this is the only one.'

I thanked her, and she stepped back and shut the door firmly in our faces.

That seemed to be the end of the inquiry. But somehow the facts did not fit. I walked away with my colleague. Was the puppy what we were looking for? Had Mrs Ballinger been a little too keen to shut the door on us? Surely we had been expecting to find an older dog showing some signs of sickness.

We went back to the house and knocked on the door again. Mrs Ballinger opened it and glared at us.

'It's not that puppy we came about,' I said to her. 'It's the older dog we want to see.'

'I haven't got another dog,' she snapped.

'We have been told that you have another dog living at your house.'

A long pause followed. 'I did have another dog,' she admitted at last.

'Where is it, then?' I asked.

'I got rid of it,' she answered.

'Well, where is it now?' I went on.

'What do you want to know for?'

I explained that we were making inquiries about a dog which had been caused unnecessary suffering.

Mrs Ballinger was silent for a minute. Then, looking directly at neither of us, she said:

'It's in the back garden. I've buried it.'

It was hardly what we had expected to hear. However, it was not enough to close the inquiry.

'If the dog is dead and you have buried it,' I told her, 'I still need to see it. It means I shall have to apply for an exhumation order so the dog can be examined by a vet.'

She protested, but I got her to sign a paper agreeing that she would allow the dog to be exhumed. I told her we would be returning as soon as we had obtained the order.

Two days later, we went back to the house, order in hand. With us were a veterinary surgeon and a supervisor from the RSPCA Animal Home. I produced the Ministry Order and we went into the garden. Mrs Ballinger showed us where to dig.

It was a young adult cross-bred bitch, sandy brown in colour. Its body was covered in sores and the skin was broken in several places. 'It smelt foul,' the supervisor from the Animal Home noted in her report. We wrapped the body in a blanket, placed it in a plastic bag and carried it away for a post-mortem examination.

The vet found a number of clear signs that the dog had been in poor physical condition for some time before its death. It had external injuries on the head, back and both front legs. There was 'extensive alopecia of the affected areas which would have been apparent during life'. Its liver was damaged, and its stomach and small intestine were completely empty of foodstuffs.

The vet concluded that the dog 'was in a state of shock at the time of death' and that it 'had been suffering for a period of some months prior to death'.

Three days after the post-mortem I went back to see Mrs Ballinger. I needed to find out how the dog had died. She had 'got rid of it', she told us at the first meeting. Now I had to establish precisely what she meant by this. Our interview was to prove a long and painful process before the grisly truth was at last unravelled, sentence by sentence.

Because she was virtually deaf, I wrote down each question for her to read before answering, and recorded her answer beneath. She signed each page of the interview and the initial caution.

After some preliminary questioning, during which she admitted that the dog was hers and that she had owned it for five months, I asked her when the dog had died.

'On the ninth of October,' she said. (That was ten days before it was exhumed for the post-mortem.)

'Why did it die?' I asked her.

'Its head was cut,' she said, and added, 'Its ribs were cut and it was cut all over.'

'Did you ever take it to a veterinary surgeon?'

'No.'

'When did you bury it?'

'That day. The day it died.'

I said to her, 'You know the dog had sores all over its body. Can you tell me how long they had been there?'

'About a week.'

I asked Mrs Ballinger about the injuries to the dog's ribs. She denied having beaten it and offered no further explanation. I put it to her that she had realised the dog was very ill, and that she had killed it and buried it in her garden.

'I did no such thing,' she protested.

'Was the dog dead when you buried it?' I asked her.

'Yes,' she replied.

I went on, 'Why did you tell me, when I first visited you, that the only dog you had was the little puppy which you still have now?'

'I did not know who you were,' she said. 'I thought you were the police.'

'How did the dog die?' I wanted to know.

She paused and nodded briefly, as if this was the one real question she had been waiting for.

'I'll tell you the truth about the dog,' she said at last. 'I was in Nottingham for a weekend. I got back on the Monday and my little girl came into me. "Brandy's ribs are all cut," she said.

'Then the girl up the road who lives at Number 35 came down. She wanted to know if the dog was all right. She said it was under her bed and that her floor was covered in blood.

'So I asked what had happened to the dog and she said she didn't know. I asked her if it was her big dog that was biting mine. Again she didn't know.

'I went outside and called the dog but it wouldn't come in for me. Then I went next door and asked the woman if she would telephone the RSPCA to come and get the dog so it could be looked after. She made the call and came out and told me the office was closed and she could only get an answering machine. Anyway, she said, they would only come out for stray dogs or dogs that were knocked down.

'So I went up to the woman's house and found the dog under her bed. I got it out and carried it home. I put her in the coal hole. I was going to bring her into town in the morning to have her put down. Then I put some water in the bath to give her a wash, because she was smelling awful.

'I lifted the dog into the water and started washing her. I was washing her and she slipped under the water. I kept washing her. I didn't know she was dead. I pulled out the plug. It was too late, the dog was dead.'

Mrs Ballinger paused, and looked at me. In a few brief words she had suggested that the dog had quietly drowned itself while she carried on washing it.

Was I really meant to believe she had not used a hand to help it slide under the water, and that she had not held it there until the dog was dead?

'When did you know it was dead?' I asked her.

'I didn't,' she said quickly. 'I thought it was still alive.'

'Yes,' she went on, as though remembering each moment as it had actually happened. 'I thought it was still alive, so I let the water out of the bath. I left the dog lying there, then I went and fetched my hair-dryer. I lifted her out to dry her, but there was no life in the dog at all.

'So then I put her in a plastic bag and wrapped her up in a blanket. I left her in a corner in the coal hole and then I went out to the garden and dug a hole. Then I dragged the dog out into it and buried it. That's all,' she concluded.

I asked her some further questions. Then I said:

'Did the dog drown?'

'Yes,' she said quickly. 'That's right. The dog drowned. Yes. That's right.' She seemed as keen to dispose of the question as she had been to get the dog out of the way, buried and forgotten.

I asked her, 'Could you not have kept the dog's head above water?'

'I washed the dog seven times in the bath,' she replied. 'The dog was too weak. She had lost a lot of blood.'

'A lot of blood?'

'Yes, that's right. The dog was weak.'

It seemed that Mrs Ballinger had prepared the elements of her story with some care. The dog was weak from loss of blood, and she had been too busy washing it to notice that its head had slipped beneath the surface of the water.

The episode with the hair-dryer was interesting. It suggested to me that in a sudden panic, as soon as she realised she had drowned the dog, she had tried to dry its fur and so efface any sign that it had been anywhere near a bath. Just then, however, I was unlikely to get her to agree to any such version of events.

I told her I had no further questions, and would be reporting the facts to my Headquarters. Mrs Ballinger said she would be consulting a solicitor.

'That would be a sensible thing to do,' I said, and left the house.

That same day I went to see a Mrs Gordon at No.35. She confirmed that the dog had been in her house. She had found it lying on her child's bed. When she went to pick it up it ran off and she had followed it back to Mrs Ballinger's house.

There Mrs Ballinger had explained the bleeding. 'It was in use,' she had said, meaning it was in season. (Something she had not mentioned to me.)

Later that night the dog returned to Mrs Gordon's house and she had chased it out. The next morning, when she opened the door, it was on her step again.

'I did not let it in,' she said, 'because it was still in a bad state and was in need of treatment, and I did not want my children to touch it.

Mrs Ballinger appeared before the Leeds Magistrates charged with causing unnecessary suffering to a dog. At the first hearing she made much of her deafness and a special session was arranged. She then, after much consultation, changed her plea to guilty.

After the evidence had been heard, the Magistrates said they thought it was a very serious case. Mrs Ballinger was given a three-month prison sentence suspended for two years. She was disqualified for life from keeping a dog. I was later told that it was only because she had a young daughter that she had been spared from going to prison.

It was a distasteful and unnecessary crime. Had she thought with any care about calling in the RSPCA, she could have done so and the dog would have been taken off her hands. But perhaps she had reservations about letting animal experts see the state she had allowed the dog to get into.

I had my own suspicions that she had beaten the dog herself. We could not prove this, partly because she had intimidated certain of her neighbours into keeping their mouths shut.

The puppy was taken away from her. This, at least, was one creature that could look forward to a better future.

A PONY IN PAIN

This was a straightforward case. A pony was being tethered out on council land on the outskirts of Leeds. It was lame and suffering from laminitis, an inflammation of the tissue covering its hooves. We prosecuted the owner for omitting to provide necessary care and attention, and she was found guilty and fined.

The case also raised other issues relevant to the plight of horses left out by themselves for long periods every day. The area where it lived was plagued by stray dogs, from which it had no protection at all, being tethered on open moorland. Young boys were another form of menace. In their free time they roamed in these fields and might suddenly do anything to a helpless animal – from throwing stones at it to jumping on its back. This again is something that impetuous would-be owners do not think about. They are in such a rush to buy the horse, they fail to consider the physical dangers to which it will be exposed if they leave it out on common land.

When I first heard about this particular pony, a grey gelding about 11 or 12 years of age, it had already been impounded by the horse wardens following a complaint by someone living near the ground where it was tethered. (In Leeds, as elsewhere in the country, the horse wardens are a token force employed by the local authority to monitor the treatment of horses in the area. At that time they were attached to the Parks Department in Leeds. In other places the dog wardens double up as horse wardens. All are underfunded and understaffed and can never really get to grips with the problems they face.)

I went to see the pony at the council's paddock in Gildersome, to the south of the city. He was obviously lame on all four legs and in considerable pain. As he walked he did not know which leg to put down first.

I called a veterinary surgeon to examine and treat the pony, and set off to make contact with the owner. She was a 24-year-old housewife, and I interviewed her next morning at the RSPCA's Animal Home in Leeds.

She confirmed that she owned the grey pony which had been taken from council land on the outskirts of Leeds. Then I asked her if she knew the pony was suffering from laminitis.

'Yes', she replied, 'and he was under treatment.'

'When did your vet last see him?' I asked.

'Tuesday 16th February,' she answered. That was two weeks ago.

'What advice did he give you?' I wanted to know.

Her answer was direct and revealing. 'He told me to get his hooves clipped. And he more or less advised me to get him shot. But I couldn't do it.'

'Why was he tethered out on council land?'

'I had nowhere else to put him,' she replied.

'How long have you had him?' I asked her.

'Eleven years.'

'Do you agree that because of his condition he should have been taken in?'

'Yes,' she said. 'But I didn't think it would have made much difference. He'd been out all his life. He is a Welsh mountain pony.'

It was the old argument. Because it was a mountain pony (or a Dartmoor or New Forest pony), it could be expected to look after itself in all weathers. I pointed out that, unlike a wild pony, her horse was not free to move where he wanted. She had kept him on a tether.

'Yes,' she replied, 'because he was not allowed any grass.'

By this she meant that the vet had warned her against letting the horse have grass because it could help bring on laminitis or make an existing case worse. In no way, though, had the vet condoned tethering out the horse.

I pressed on. I said to her, 'But he could not get any shelter from the prevailing wind, could he?'

'There were bushes near him,' she replied.

It was a defiant answer. I guessed she made it mainly to protect her wounded pride, her failure to keep the horse in good health. The bushes she mentioned, as I checked later on a visit to the tethering ground, could offer little to a horse. The whole area was open bleak scrubland, quite unsuitable for a tethered animal.

That was the end of the interview. I told the woman that I was not satisfied that she had cared for her horse in the correct manner by leaving him tethered out, exposed to all weathers, while he was in poor physical condition. I would be reporting the facts of the case, I advised her. For the time being the horse would remain in the council paddock.

The vet's report confirmed my misgivings. He diagnosed that the animal was suffering from chronic laminitis which made it reluctant to walk. It was in a fair degree of pain, the report went on, and the vet added:

'Further examination revealed that all four soles of the feet had "dropped". In my opinion this horse has been caused unnecessary pain and suffering, by cause of neglect.'

I made my report to RSPCA Headquarters in Horsham, stating also that I had spoken to the owner's vet. He agreed with our own vet's diagnosis and said that the horse should have been taken in. He felt, too, that he should have been called again to examine it. He also told me that he would not support the owner in court.

HQ had reservations about proceeding with the case, partly because a vet had been consulted only two weeks before the animal was impounded. It was the kind of fact that might make magistrates sympathetic to the owner.

I could see what they meant. However, I persisted with my view that the owner had failed to follow specific advice given by her veterinary surgeon and that because of this the animal was caused considerable suffering. HQ agreed, and instructed me to pursue the case in court, laying a charge of causing unnecessary suffering to the grey gelding.

No mention of tethering was made in the charge, since the RSPCA's vet had not indicated that the manner of tethering had contributed to the animal's suffering. Nonetheless, I hoped that the publicity arising from the case would help in dissuading future horse owners from leaving their animals tethered out. The case was heard the following July, four months after the pony was impounded. The woman pleaded not guilty but was found guilty by the bench. Her vet declined to support her in court, and she was fined £125, ordered to pay vets' fees of £86.25 and solicitors' fees of £175. She was ordered to pay these amounts at £5 per week.

To an extent the case was a success. We had proved our point about the animal's suffering and the owner had been punished. For me, however, the chief aim had been to do something to help the cause of tethered horses, and in this we had made little progress. It was not, it seemed, enough of a controversial issue. On present evidence, it is difficult to see why the authorities, and ultimately the Government, are content to let the *status quo* continue.

In Leeds and Bradford the RSPCA receive many complaints from members of the public concerned about the welfare of tethered horses. To this end Leeds City Council proposed the introduction of a bye-law which would make tethering illegal on council land. It was refused. Until some other form of decisive action is brought into play, the animals will continue to suffer.

BIRDS TAKEN FROM
THE WILD

In my West Yorkshire region we had a rash of teenagers and young men going out and stealing young wild birds from their nests. To catch them, we mounted a special combined operation of RSPCA and police officers (which colleagues nicknamed the 'Flying Squad'). The police took out search warrants and we raided a number of houses at the same time.

The raids yielded several owls, kestrels and other birds which we confiscated and later released into the wild. We took the boys to court, and also their parents for aiding and abetting them by allowing various garden sheds to be used for keeping the birds.

One of the mothers used an ingenious line of defence to protect herself. When asked why she had allowed her son to keep a bird which he had unlawfully taken, she told the Magistrate:

'I thought it was a budgie he had in there. It wasn't till I saw that advertisement on television, you know, for the lager, that I realised it was a kestrel.'

I'm happy to say that she did not get away with it!

In the case I am about to describe, we had received reports that a young man was keeping a fledgling owl at his house. Accompanied by two RSPCA colleagues I went to his house in Bradford.

The young man was making no attempt to hide what he was doing. We found him in his front garden standing next to a fledgling Tawny Owl which was perching on a barrel.

I told him why we had come, and that it was an offence to take and keep an owl.

'Yes, I know,' he replied.

I cautioned him and asked him where he had obtained the owl.

'Got it from a friend three weeks ago,' he said. 'He told me he'd got it from the woods but I didn't believe him.'

I asked him if he went looking for birds.

'I go with a friend,' he replied. 'He does the taxidermist stuff and sells them. If anyone wants owt, he'll do it.'

I told him that he should not be in possession of the owl. He was imprinting it in a way that was not helpful to it. I said I wanted to take the owl away and have an expert prepare it to be returned to its natural state. He agreed and one of my colleagues took the owl and placed it in one of our vans. Before we left, I said that I would be reporting the facts to my Headquarters.

I sent in my report to HQ and they agreed that the young man should be prosecuted. He was charged as follows:

'That he did have in his possession a certain live wild bird, namely a Tawny Owl, contrary to Section 1(2)(a) of the Wildlife and Countryside Act 1981.

The case was heard at Bradford Magistrates' Court. The defendant was found guilty and fined £75 – an impressive amount compared with some fines for cruelty offences against animals. I hoped it would keep his nose out of bird's nests until he saw sense.

A PUPPY FARMING CASE

During my period working in Wales I had been watching Evan Thomas for some while. He lived on a run-down farm which he kept in a disgusting state. He bred and dealt in dogs, selling them on to pet shops in the Birkenhead and Crewe areas. He also supplied animals to companies which used them for experimental purposes. He had no licences to cover any of his trading activities.

He openly advertised in the local newspaper. In one issue he offered to buy unwanted cats. The same issue carried this notice, in English and Welsh:

BREEDING OF DOGS ACT 1973

The Breeding of Dogs Act, 1973 came into force on 1st April, 1974, and its main purpose is to regulate the commercial breeding of dogs. The Council is empowered to inspect premises and exercise control over the transportation of puppies.

No person may keep a breeding establishment for dogs without a licence granted by a local authority. A breeding establishment is any premises where more than two bitches are kept for the purpose of breeding for sale.

An application form for the said licence is obtainable from the undersigned officer and should be completed and returned before the 29th June, 1974. Further information and advice may be obtained from the Director of Public Health and Housing, Council Offices,....

Two years later I was still vainly trying to persuade that same

District Council to take action against people who, simply by ignoring the existence of the new Act, could apparently do what they liked with no fear of punishment or retribution. In that time, if the council had clamped down on Evan Thomas and numerous other unscrupulous breeders, they would have saved countless animals from distress and suffering.

They did nothing. Call it obstinacy, a cowboy mentality, an inbred hatred of change or what you will, these people nevertheless had obligations under the law and I was determined to make them admit their responsibilities, and start taking offenders to court.

It was easier said than done, and I had few allies to call on. I was beginning to feel depressed as well as frustrated. Maybe, I thought, I was overreacting to the new law. Maybe, if I just left them alone for a while, they would see sense and come round of their own accord.

That was nonsense, of course, and in my heart I knew it. Unless the councillors were continually prodded, they would never do anything. As I have mentioned, not a few of these respected citizens were themselves involved in the puppy racket – mainly as breeders and dealers, though there were others on the fringe, who had a professional interest in seeing to it that the *status quo* was not disturbed by 'inconvenient' new laws.

One of my most important allies was the local Diseases of Animals Inspector. It was our visit to Thomas's kennels that finally gave us the irrefutable evidence we needed.

We had worked together at the horse and cattle markets in the area. Now I asked him for his help and he agreed to come with me to visit Evan Thomas.

At ten o'clock on that Friday morning, we entered Thomas's property and stared about us in disbelief. It was like a battlefield. Carcases and bones lay strewn about the place. Dogs roamed free among the household junk which littered the yard and helped themselves to what rotting meat they could find. An old beagle gnawed on the exposed ribs of a decaying sheep. A sheepdog tugged at the severed leg of a calf. Next to an old van, used for housing dogs, lay several carcases of sheep in various stages of decomposition. Close to the farmhouse, a pile of about twenty carcases lay stacked in a rough heap. The smell from this pile was nauseating.

Thomas had not so far put in an appearance. He would have a lot of explaining to do when he did show up. Even by his previous standards, the farm had sunk to a new level of horror: it was like a concentration camp for animals. Worse still, we realised, it was health hazard of major proportions. Disease could easily spread from here to other farms in the area.

I contacted the police, the Ministry Vets, the Environmental Health Department, and an independent veterinary surgeon who would provide a report for the RSPCA. In due course, officers from each of the official departments came to the farm. One of them took photographs of the scene.

When Thomas finally decided to show himself, I told him that the carcases must be cleared up at once. One of the officers added that he would be reported for failing to bury dead animals.

I did a rough count of the puppies and dogs living at the farm. It came to about forty, of varying breeds and ages. I asked Thomas what he did with all these dogs. He sold them, he said. Some went to pet shops and others to a company dealing in animal experimentation.

I asked him if he was registered under the Pet Animals Act. No, he replied. I told him he would have to register if he wished to carry on his business. I pointed out to him that if he had two or more bitches and was breeding for sale, he would also have to obtain a licence under the Breeding of Dogs Act. His reply staggered me. No, he said, he had not applied because he thought his farm would not meet the standards required. Those standards were for rich people, he added.

I warned him again that he would be reported to the local authority for the offences he had already committed. Meanwhile, he must clear up the carcases and get rid of them.

The following Monday I went back to the kennels. This time there was not a bone or carcase in sight. For the rest, little had changed. I was not at all satisfied with the way Thomas was housing the dogs – basically in a concrete hut with no exercise yard – and told him so. He replied that he was going to sell off some of his stock and not buy in any more. I told him again that he needed to apply for licences to breed and sell dogs. I would come back soon, I said, to check on the welfare of the dogs.

Almost two months later I returned to Thomas's kennels with

two policemen and an independent vet. As we approached the farm we met Evan Thomas coming towards us. He could not see us today, he said. He was going off for a meal and did not want to come back afterwards. I made an appointment with him for three days later.

With the same three men, I went to the puppy farm again. The vet asked to examine the animals, and later in his report listed a total of 51. In his own words they were described as follows:

1 adult working Collie
1 Corgi dog, male
5 cross-bred Sheepdogs under six months
1 aged Poodle bitch
1 Poodle, male, over six months
2 Beagles, matron bitches
1 Yorkshire Terrier over six months
1 Golden Cocker Spaniel, male adult
2 Old English bitches, year-old and five year-old
1 Terrier bitch, three year-old
1 Beagle, aged dog
1 Sheepdog, two year-old bitch
1 Old English Sheepdog, two year-old bitch
1 Old English Sheepdog bitch, nine months old
1 Samoyed bitch, adult
2 Sheepdogs, under six months old
3 Dachshunds, matron bitch, year-old bitch, year-old male
1 Retriever bitch, year-old
1 Terrier, three year-old male
1 Old English, seven year-old bitch
1 Yorkie, mother of seven week-old litter
7 Yorkie pups
1 Black and White Spaniel, six year-old
1 Sheepdog bitch, one and a half year-old
3 matron Dachshund bitches, varying ages
1 Spaniel bitch rearing puppies
8 Spaniel puppies, two weeks-old.

The list is revealing in several ways. It shows a large number of dogs of different breeds, many breeding bitches and 15 puppies in two litters. It is typical of the mass-production approach of so many puppy farmers. It matters little to them which breed they produce.

Saleable bodies are what they want – as many and as fast as possible.

The vet found that the dogs were 'in satisfactory bodily condition and free from external parasites.' He also examined the main kennel building and found it suitable only for sleeping quarters. Although most of the dogs were kept in this block, there was no exercise yard for them. The vet had further complaints:

'Kennel refuse was heaped up against the end wall outside the building. The need for proper faeces and bedding disposal was stressed. Old tyres, bins and plastic bags littered the surrounding area. This would provide vermin with ideal shelter ...'

Two chicken-house types of wooden shed housed the two litters mentioned. Whilst this might have been acceptable to an owner with one or two bitches, with plenty of time to concentrate on them, it was not satisfactory as a breeding department in an establishment that had 51 dogs.

In his conclusions the vet stated:

'The facilities on this holding are quite unsuitable for the number of dogs kept at present. They are positively unsuitable for breeding purposes. The owner maintained he wasn't breeding, but two litters were seen on the premises and many of the brood bitches showed signs of a life-time of breeding – as evidenced by their large low-slung mammary glands.'

While the vet was examining the dogs, I spoke to the puppy farmer. Did he know how many dogs he had? I asked.

'You tell me,' came the answer.

I told him that I felt he was committing offences under the Pet Animals Act 1951 and the Breeding of Dogs Act 1973 and cautioned him. I asked him: 'Have you got a licence under the Pet Animals Act 1951?'

'No,' he replied.

'Have you applied to the local authority?'

'No,' he said, 'I didn't really know about it.'

'Have you applied for a licence under the Breeding of Dogs Act 1973?'

'No, not yet,' he said.

I told him he would be reported. He answered, 'I'll have to do something now.'

It all seemed cut and dried. I collected statements from the police, the vet, added my own and submitted these to the District Council. Again, although we had more than enough to begin proceedings against Thomas, the council did nothing.

Weeks went by and it looked as though I was beating my head against a brick wall. Close to despair, I went to the police in Aberystwyth. A Chief Inspector there listened carefully, and when I had finished my tale of woe offered me the first encouragement I had heard in ages. 'Stick to your guns,' he said. 'Don't give in to these people.'

He went on to say that he felt I had a worthwhile case and was prepared to support me as much as he could. He kept his word. After a meeting with his superior officer, it was decided that the police would take on the case.

Thomas was accused on 11 charges, nine of them for permitting the carcases of seven sheep, a calf and a pig to remain unburied in a yard to which dogs had access. Charge No.10 was for 'failing to have a licence as required under the Pet Animals Act 1951'. Charge No.11 was for 'failing to have a licence as required by the Breeding of Dogs Act 1973'. Although the latter Act had been in force for almost two and a half years, this was the first time a charge under its provisions had been brought in the county of Dyfed.

The case was heard at Aberystwyth Magistrates Court. Evan Thomas appeared in court and pleaded not guilty to all charges.

The solicitor representing Thomas brought as a witness the Environmental Health Officer who had visited the farm on behalf of the local authority. To our amazement, he stated that he did not think there was a health hazard at the farm:

'Although the conditions were pretty bad, with dead animals about the place,' he said, 'I feel there was no danger to public health due to the remoteness of the smallholding.'

How he could make such a claim defied belief, in our view, because crows and other birds could pick up infected meat and drop it in other fields in the surrounding area.

The Magistrates, however, took a different view from that of the officer. They considered the police photographs of the scene and found Thomas guilty on all of the first nine charges. He was fined £5 on each. The maximum fine available at the time for that offence was £10.

On Charge No.10 he was found guilty and fined £5. He was

lucky, in that the maximum fine was then £25 and might also be combined with imprisonment for up to three months.

When Charge No.11 was heard, Thomas tried to make the court believe that he used only two bitches to breed from, and his solicitor made great play on this point. Thomas fared less well under cross-examination. Time and again the prosecuting barrister had him admitting that other bitches at the farm had given birth to puppies which he had sold.

The veterinary surgeon who had examined the dogs on one of our visits to the farm, gave his statement. His view, quoted earlier, that 'many of the brood bitches showed signs of a life-time of breeding' carried telling weight. The magistrates found Evan Thomas guilty on this charge too. He was fined £20 and ordered to pay £10 in costs.

For the police and myself it was a victory not only this particular puppy farmer but also against the local authority. Until the case was brought, they had consistently refused to take action when they must have known it was their duty to do so. Then, in court, the Environmental Health Officer had tried to have the charges dismissed, saying that only the local authority had the right to institute proceedings in a case of this kind. The Magistrates disagreed, and countered by asking why the local authority had not acted. This caused a number of red faces among council observers.

However, any satisfaction I may have derived directly from the case was short-lived. Days later I heard that the Licensing Committee had met to consider Evan Thomas's applications for licences to breed dogs and deal in them. They were approved, and Thomas became instantly free to carry on as though nothing had happened. He was £80 out of pocket, but the proceeds from selling just three puppies would easily cover that.

The case of Evan Thomas brought several skeletons out of the cupboard. It demonstrated scandalous neglect in the treatment of animals. It showed the mind-boggling complacency of local councillors charged with awarding licences to breed and sell dogs.

More scandalous still, the puppy farmers are just as active today as they were a dozen years ago. No one seems to have learned a single thing.

SUFFERING ON THE FARM :
MORRIS VERSUS MORRIS

Letter addressed to 'The Local Inspector of Cruelty to Animals':

> Dear Sir,
> I wish to inform you that I have young calves being starve
> (*sic*) to death, because of the stubborn attitude of my sister's
> solicitor, refusing to pay creditors. There is plenty of money
> in the Bank but they will not release it, and because of it not
> one of my usual suppliers will supply with calf-cake. Rather
> than starving these calves to death, I decided to report the fact
> to you sir. So please call on me at your earliest convenience,
> which I consider very urgent indeed.
> Yours faithfully,
> P.L. Morris

The letter had a formal business heading and the address, Valley
Farm. It was my introduction to an extraordinary saga. At its root
was a long-standing feud between Peter Morris (the letter writer)
and his sister Barbara.

Members of the Morris family owned two neighbouring farms.
Meadow Farm was wholly owned by Peter Morris and he looked
after it well. The cause of the trouble was Valley Farm, which was
jointly owned by Peter and Barbara Morris. Until his death ten
years earlier there had been a second brother, and during his
lifetime all three owned an equal share in the farm.

From gossip at the cattle market I learned that the three hated
each other, and constantly formed alliances of two versus one,
always the sister with one brother against the other. This continued
until the second brother died and left his entire share to his sister
Barbara. She then moved away to a smallholding some distance
away, leaving her brother Peter to run Valley Farm. However, as

senior partner with a two-thirds interest in the farm, she insisted that Peter Morris should submit all bills to her and that she should countersign all cheques issued on the 'Morris Bros.' farm account.

Subservience to his sister – who, at 58, was seven years younger than himself – was more than Peter Morris could bear. By the time I arrived on the scene, he was becoming erratic and depressed, and could no longer bring himself to speak directly to his sister. She, in turn, appeared to be afraid of him and was careful to keep her distance, living 40 miles away and never going near the shared property.

It was no way to run a farm. In the months following Morris's introductory letter, I went to see him several times, encouraging and persuading him to keep going. I made contact with his sister, both directly by telephone and through her solicitor and accountant. I reminded her of her responsibilities as a partner in the farm. Although it was clear that, on her side too, the brother-sister relationship had developed some hideous tangles, she did agree that her brother could sell some livestock and buy food with the proceeds to feed the remaining animals. In December her solicitor confirmed this in writing.

By now I was keeping an almost constant watch on the farm. Mr Morris was still failing to feed the cattle at Valley Farm at the proper intervals – although the cattle at his own farm were well cared for.

Things came to a head on early in January. I went to Valley Farm one morning and Mr Morris took me to a barn where I found two calves that were down and unable to stand, and one that was dead. I told Mr Morris of my concern for all the animals at Valley. I would return later in the day with a veterinary surgeon, I advised him. If he wished to arrange for his own vet to be present, he was entitled to do so.

That evening I went again to the farm, together with the vet. He took blood and faeces samples from a number of animals, and with Peter Morris's permission destroyed a three-month-old calf which was weakened and emaciated beyond recall. In his report he wrote, 'This was one of a batch of young calves weaned onto a bulky, fibrous diet which their digestive systems, owing to their immaturity, were unable to cope with.'

While the vet went about his work, Peter Morris told me he was sorry the animals were suffering but if his sister would let him he would buy her out. He would give her a cheque the same day, and all this suffering would stop. I replied that he had to find some solution to the problem. His sister had given him permission to sell some of the stock to buy food. Why did he not do so? He replied that he would not even consider the idea.

The vet and I left the farm. A week later we went back to check on the animals. Five more calves had died from lack of proper food. I asked Mr Morris for an explanation. After being cautioned, he made this statement:

'I have lost 6 calves under a week, 9 calves 1 to 5 months old. The reason for this is by being unable to buy balanced food concentrates necessary for that age group. I am in a position where I can pay for food but my money is tied up and it is a matter of dispute with my sister. I have 30 to 40 calves due in the next two months and I have not sufficient food to see me through the winter. The reason for not buying food is that the bank is determined to wind up the partnership affair. I as an expert in livestock husbandry regret that these animals have had to suffer because of the unco-operative attitude of my sister.'

The vet, in his report, amplified the reasons why the young calves were dying:

'Available food supplies were silage, hay and barley. With this low-protein, fibrous diet the early weaned calves would be the class of stock mainly affected. Whereas adult stock would survive on such a diet with only a reduction in milk yield and loss of flesh, in young calves it means chronic indigestion, debility, emaciation and death.'

He added that he felt Mr Morris's failure to provide a satisfactory, balanced diet amounted to causing unnecessary suffering. He also felt bound to comment on the farmer's repeated pleas that his hands were tied because of a family disagreement.

'I warned him,' wrote the vet, 'that the suffering of the cattle should not be used as a lever in a family argument and that "suffering" was "suffering" no matter what the cause might happen to be.'

It was clear that we would have to bring a prosecution. I reported the facts to RSPCA Headquarters and arranged for a colleague of mine to call on Miss Barbara Morris. He obtained her official admission that she was a partner in the farm and warned her that she would be reported for causing unnecessary suffering to a number of calves.

HQ considered the case and ruled that we should prosecute Peter Morris by himself. The fact that a few months ago the sister had sent a letter through her solicitor, authorising the sale of livestock to feed the other animals, would make it difficult to secure a conviction against her.

After two adjournments, the case was heard in March. Peter Morris pleaded guilty and was fined a small amount plus costs. It was not much, but the main thing was that the Magistrates in this stoutly reactionary part of the world had found a local farmer guilty of ill-treating one of his animals. In my report to HQ, I could not refrain from adding this slightly cynical footnote:

'To obtain even a small amount from this particular bench is an achievement in itself.'

The conviction had a positive effect ... for the time being. Peter Morris resumed proper feeding at Valley Farm and it seemed that brother and sister had reached some kind of workable arrangement. Nine months passed, then the following December I received a letter from Miss Morris.

She complained that her brother had separated their joint herd into two parts, representing her two-thirds share and his one-third. He was leaving her share out in the top field and had said that he was not going to milk them, nor would he let her remove her share from the farm.

I tried to contact both of them by telephone but received no answer. Sensing a new emergency I got in touch with the vet, and together that afternoon we visited the farm. Daylight was beginning to fade when we arrived, and Peter Morris was nowhere to be found. We set off on a long tour of inspection, locating as many cattle as we could and checking their condition. Valley Farm is one of the largest farms in the area and the cattle were widely dispersed. Fortunately, all the animals we found were in fair condition and not in need of milking.

I finally came across a cowhand at the farm. He said he knew the old dispute between the Morrises was hotting up again. So far as he was concerned, he had orders to milk only those cows that Mr Morris collected for him each day. The vet and I left the farm and

I filed a report, promising to keep in touch with events at the farm.

Christmas went by, then at the turn of the year I heard from the farm foreman. He was worried, he told me. The only food available for the cattle was silage. He had nothing else to give them and Mr Morris refused to take any further responsibility for the animals. He had announced that he had given up all work on the farm, then locked himself in a garage and refused to come out.

I went up to the farm with the vet and a police constable. Animals I can take care of, but distressed humans are not strictly my business; hence the policeman.

The farm foreman showed us to the garage where Peter Morris was holed up. The building had a side door with a letterbox which offered the only means of talking to Morris without shouting through a wall. As I peered through the letterbox and tried to reason with him, I could not actually see him, and for a long time he refused to speak. I kept on talking, and at last he could hold back no longer. The words rushed from him like a sudden release of floodwater through a weir. The gist of it all was:

'It's nothing to do with me! I take no further responsibility for this farm! My foreman is in charge! If you want to know something, talk to him ...' The ranting went on and on until, too frustrated to continue, the voice stopped.

As we prepared to leave the farm, the foreman told me how unhappy he and the other farmworkers were about the situation. They no longer knew if they were going to be paid, and they were sorry about the animals. But, what could they do? I promised to speak to Miss Morris and see what could be sorted out for them.

That evening I telephoned Miss Barbara Morris and told her that her brother was behaving strangely; he was very likely unwell and was refusing to look after the farm. She was most unhelpful. She claimed there was nothing she could do. Anyway, her brother was only sulking, she said; that was all it was. I said that as a partner in the farm business she had a responsibility to manage its affairs when the other partner was ill. This she flatly denied.

I rang off. Having got nowhere with her, I later rang the police and next day arrangements were made for a social worker to visit Valley Farm and speak to Peter Morris.

Speak to him she did, through the letterbox, but got no reply for her pains. Nor did a local GP fare much better. Later, in his surgery, he told me that, although he had not actually seen Morris during his stint at the letterbox, he was happy that he was physically and mentally all right.

In the next few days I made regular visits to the farm to check, as best I could, on Morris and the animals. I kept Miss Morris up to date with her brother's condition and spoke also to her accountant who acted as a mediator between the warring sister and brother.

At last, on 9 January, a breakthrough happened at the farm. Morris finally agreed to open the garage door and let me talk to him face to face.

I could have used a clothes peg on my nose when I went in there. Morris, more stubbly and wild-looking than ever, scuttled back to his bed as I entered the garage. He wore an old vest and nothing else. The bed was a mattress he had hauled in from somewhere and covered with blankets.

Peter Morris's decision to give up on life had not been taken on the spur of the moment. The day before, he had driven into town and bought several boxes of Main Course soup. This had been his sole diet for the last nine days, eaten cold from the tin. He had not budged from the garage in that time. The small rectangular space served as his toilet as well as his bedroom, and it stank from heaven to breakfast.

As we began to speak, Morris had little to add to the debate beyond heaping all the blame on his sister. He asked me to write out a letter for him. It was for his sister, he said, would I take it to her? I agreed to do so. Still lying in bed, he dictated these words to me:

'I want to confirm that as from midnight 31st December I am no longer responsible for the cattle. I hereby give my sister, Miss Barbara Elizabeth Morris, permission to dispose of all the cattle as she wishes and authorise Inspector Jenkins to act on my behalf in speaking to my sister.' He signed the letter 'P.L. Morris', and added to me that 'she must take the lot'.

I told him I would deliver the letter to his sister. Before I left the farm, I said, was there anything I could do to help prevent the animals from suffering any more hardship? Lying there in his raggedy bed, Morris did not want to talk about the animals, and did not reply.

Was he all right in himself? I asked. He grunted and said he had hurt his back, but he refused my offer to get a doctor to call on him. In his mind, I could see, he was still going over the row with his sister and the letter he had just given me.

'I've made up my mind about this,' he said suddenly, looking past me at the door. Then he repeated his vow to give up his responsibility for the partnership. He went on:

'I gave two months' notice to her and the solicitors. No-one knows the value of freedom until you have lost it, and I would rather walk the roads as a tramp than start next year in partnership with her.'

His mention of freedom explained a great deal. Ever since the death of his brother, I guessed, he had felt trapped by the partnership arrangement, in particular at having less say ultimately than his sister. He had tried to buy her out and she had refused. Now he wanted to get out completely, to be free of her. To make sure I had got the point, he looked at me now and said:

'I own only a one-third share of the farm. Two-thirds belongs to my sister. Therefore the overall responsibility is hers. I give authority for cattle to be sold to cover the writ. I can't be more fair than that.'

Next day I went to interview Miss Morris in the presence of her accountant. I told her what was going on at the two farms, and what her brother wanted to do to resolve their problems. I showed her his letter.

Miss Morris read the letter carefully, nodded and handed it to her accountant, who also read it. Then she gave her verdict. She would agree to sell the cattle. The accountant would get in touch at once with the auctioneers to arrange the sale. In the meantime, food for the animals would be provided as soon as possible.

I went back to see Peter Morris and tell him the news. He seemed happy enough about the way his sister had at last fallen in with his wishes. I left him at the farm and returned to Aberystwyth. With any luck, I thought, this will see the end of the battle between the co-proprietors of Morris Bros.

I should have known better. Within days, Peter Morris had changed his mind. When a representative from the auctioneers called to gather details for the sale catalogue, he refused to let him on the farm. I also learned that Miss Morris had indeed ordered cattle food for Valley Farm, to be delivered; but when the truck arrived at the farm, it was turned back by someone acting on Mr Morris's instructions.

For me and the trusty local vet the bell had sounded for a new round of intervention at Valley Farm, and at Meadow Farm too. On Saturday 17 January we went first to Morris's own farm and found 12 calves in the cowshed that looked in poor condition. Outside, under cover, 17 yearlings stood six inches deep in slurry; they were lowing and in some distress. We went over to Valley Farm and found heifers also standing in slurry, with no dry place to lie down. One of the farmhands told me that Peter Morris had forbidden any milking to be done at the weekend. Although this order had not been carried out on that particular Saturday, it was something we would have to be wary of in future weeks.

Three days later, a mix-up over who would pay for the cattle food order led to the supplier receiving a hostile telephone call from Peter Morris. He would take a gun to anyone, auctioneer or otherwise, who went near his cattle, he shouted. Under no circumstances did he want any foodstuffs delivered.

Knowing that a lot of Morris's outbursts had a large component of hot air in them, I tried again to persuade him to look after his livestock better and to see they were properly fed. He refused. Whether I liked it or not, I was going to have to accept that we were in for weeks of trouble, probably leading to another court case.

Morris and his sister were as incompatible as any two people I have met. Sometimes you can visit a couple who are in conflict, and sit round a table and talk to them. Outwardly, they will try to be civilised and talk about their difficulties – even though, inwardly, they may be kicking each other. The Morrises were far worse. They would not even enter the same house, let alone sit round a table together.

Again I tried to switch Morris's mind to his professional duties as a farmer, but all I got from him was a lot of babble about his family problems. 'You must understand,' he cried, 'that this is a war to end all wars.'

I had had enough. A farmer who refuses to farm is a public menace. I cautioned him and told him he would be reported. His response was to make a statement. As ever, the keynote was political. It read:

'It breaks my heart to withdraw my management but I had to do it for the animals' sake and nothing more. It is terrible that I have to do this because of my sister's refusal to countersign cheques. On the advice of my bank manager I have no other course to take because he advised me that the sole ambition of my sister was to ruin me and the business.'

Having got that off his chest, he said he was prepared to look after the cattle provided his sister guaranteed to start negotiating a settlement with him. He was like a child or a madman, sometimes I could not decide which. He certainly preferred talking to action. I persuaded him at least to accept delivery of the cattle food and to allow his men to feed the animals. Later in the week I went to see Miss Morris. I told her I was not satisfied with the arrangements for looking after the cattle at Valley Farm. I cautioned her and told her she would be reported for failing to provide necessary care and attention to her animals. Although foodstuffs had been delivered, I warned her, there was no bedding-down straw at the farm and the food supply would not last beyond the weekend.

Meanwhile the vet, in his latest report, emphasised the urgency of '(i) getting supplementary feeding in for the younger stock, and (ii) getting yards and pens cleared of muck so that the animals could at least lie on dry concrete floors.'

You may wonder what the Ministry Vets were doing to help during this whole saga. The short answer is that as far as I was concerned they were useless. I called them out to Valley Farm and they came on a couple of occasions. They showed little interest and did nothing.

There was calm for a week. Then on 31 January I took a phone call from the police. Peter Morris had called at the police station to inform everyone that he had withdrawn his labour, and his men had done the same. There would be no milking or feeding of the animals on either of his farms.

I contacted Miss Morris, and patiently explained her brother's latest move. Again she refused to accept responsibility. No, she said, she would not come to Valley Farm and see the animals for herself. That evening I went with the vet and a policeman to the farms. At Meadow Farm we found that the dairy cows had been milked but the housed yearlings were hungry and noisy. At Valley Farm, although there was no milk in the bulk tank, the foreman assured me that the dairy herd was not suffering through failure to milk. Here too the housed yearlings were hungry and noisy and had no access to foodstuffs of any kind.

Next evening we returned to Valley Farm. As we approached the farm, we found a stray yearling on the road – never a good sign. We turned it into the farmyard and located Mr Morris. I told him of my concern for the housed animals that he was not feeding. He expressed surprise that the cows at Meadow Farm had been milked and made another long-winded statement, in which he admitted:

'I do not know whether or not the men will be in next week ... I will throw a bit of straw. I can't cut silage because of my back. The boy at Meadow Farm is working on his conscience if he is feeding his animals.' He also promised to meet his sister to sort out their problems. I told him he would be reported. Before leaving, I advised him of the animal we had found on the road and he said he would take care of it.

The following day, at noon, the vet and I again visited Valley Farm. In his report, the vet noted the following:

'The yearling we had turned off the road the previous evening had been left wandering about the yard and had fallen into the slurry pit during the night. She was cold and in a state of collapse ... the water system had frozen up, and water was being carried to the yearling cattle. Permission was granted for me to go round the farms to see the outlying cattle. The ones at Valley numbered about 24 ... the land they grazed was in an exposed position, very short of grass ... aggravated by the winds and icy conditions. These were tucked-up and empty-bellied to the point of being "greyhound-looking". They were pathetically short of food and Mr Morris, who had accompanied us, was told he must start feeding these immediately. This he agreed to do.

'A total of 42 yearlings were seen on the fields at Meadow Farm. These were quite contented, had more sheltered grazing and a much larger acreage to graze. By the soft, rich green faeces they were passing I felt these were being fed silage, though in previous discussions no-one would admit to this.'

The vet concluded that the outliers at Valley Farm were being caused suffering through lack of food, as were the housed yearlings at both farms. We again warned Mr Morris that he must feed his animals and keep on doing so.

That afternoon I drove to see Miss Barbara Morris. She made a statement agreeing to spend money on food provided her brother sold cattle to pay for it. 'I can't go up to see the cattle,' she said, 'because my brother is there. If he was away for a period I would co-operate in all ways.' She nevertheless agreed to attend a meeting with him in Carmarthen, at which advisers to both sides would also be present.

The eternal messenger, I drove back to Aberarth and conveyed the news to Mr Morris. He thanked me and said he would attend.

Probably he had no intention of doing so, and sure enough the planned meeting failed to take place. I contacted RSPCA Headquarters and they agreed to press ahead with charges. Although by 8 February, a week later, conditions at both farms had improved, I was still not satisfied and the next day Peter and Barbara Morris were issued with summonses to appear at the local Magistrates' Court, charged with causing unnecessary suffering to cattle.

The cases were heard on 23 February by a special Court. Miss Morris was found not guilty but Peter Morris was found guilty on two charges and fined a small amount on each plus costs. At one stage the bench had considered banning Morris from keeping animals, but then felt unable to do so.

Expenses for the RSPCA included several vet's bills, a bill for calf-rearing nuts and another for 30 bales of straw which I had provided to tide the animals over.

I found the verdicts of the Magistrates discouraging. I had spent 18 months on the case and we had still got nowhere towards improving conditions on the farms.

My report to HQ on the Court case contained another acid final paragraph. It was becoming a habit. I wrote:

'In conclusion of this report, may I thank all concerned for the advice and assistance given in this case, and now armed with this experience I will keep watch and start all over again.'

Each episode in the Morris saga followed a regular cyclical pattern. Peace between the two of them, enforced in February or March by the Courts, lasted until the onset of winter, when further hostilities broke out. Peter Morris would then announce that he could carry on no longer – 'What can I do with this daft sister of mine?' was his common refrain. Lacking any help from the Ministry Vets, I foresaw that I would again have to intervene for the RSPCA, get the animals fed and prepare for yet another court case.

In October, fearing the usual, I filed a preliminary report. Miss Barbara Morris had already been on to me, complaining that her brother had withdrawn his services and would not milk the cows. I visited the farms and was satisfied that none of the animals was suffering. I contacted Miss Morris, told her this and strongly advised her to terminate the partnership. It was the only way to ensure a lasting peace.

I knew the two sides were open to some kind of financial settlement and had been encouraging Peter Morris to make his sister an offer to buy out her two-thirds share. He did some sums and eventually came up with a proposal.

Unfortunately, when Miss Morris's advisers came back with a perfectly reasonable request to see valuations of the farm, and of the livestock and deadstock, and up-to-date accounts, Peter Morris blew up and refused to co-operate. Negotiations came to a halt.

On the farms, the animals were fed, watered and milked with tolerable efficiency until early December. By the 14th of that month, however, we again had a real crisis on our hands.

My first warning came when Peter Morris telephoned. He could no longer milk his cows, he announced abruptly. He had had an accident.

That evening I went to Valley Farm with the vet. We inspected the herd and the vet reported that 'seven of these had engorged udders to the point where there was positive suffering'.

The cows had evidently missed three milkings. They were in considerable pain and had to be milked without delay. I helped the vet to set the milking machine going and he milked out the seven cows.

The job was finished at one o'clock in the morning. I went over to Meadow Farm and told Mr Morris that the animals had suffered through lack of milking. What was his explanation? Under caution he then made this statement:

'I got up at six o'clock on Monday morning, 13th December. I then went across to Valley Farm to milk. I milked the cows as usual. I was just going to put the machine on cow 150 when she kicked back and I fell back and knocked my head on the parlour wall. I am sure I was dazed for half an hour and when the boy came at 8.15 he helped me up ...

'As regards tomorrow morning there is no-one to milk the cows at Valley. I am not fit enough myself as I cannot bend.'

Next day, after a fruitless round of telephone conversations with Miss Morris and her accountant and an equally unprofitable visit to Meadow Farm, I went to the Police Station. There I called the vet and asked him to come to Valley Farm and bring with him an experienced cowman. I would meet him there.

At noon I arrived at Meadow Farm in the company of two policemen. I had managed to persuade the police that the Morris affair had gone too far for the RSPCA alone to deal with. They agreed and I felt relief that someone else would take the initiative, at least for a day or so.

Peter Morris was cautioned and advised that he knew he had caused unnecessary suffering to seven cows by not milking them. Morris agreed, but said he was powerless. It was his sister's fault if she would not help, but the whole thing was hopeless.

'My workers won't have anything to do with my sister,' he burst out. 'My workers said in August that they were finishing this winter. I was kicked Monday morning and was out for three-quarters of an hour. My back hurts and is terribly bruised. I can't do anything about the cows.'

After further questioning, Morris was told that the facts would be reported. He shouted back:

'If that's your attitude, go on, go on then, take me to Swansea. I don't care, take me to Swansea now if you like!'

We left Morris to his dreams of prison life in Swansea and went over to Valley Farm to wait for the vet and his cowman. They arrived at 13.15 and we all helped to bring in the herd, a total of 62 Friesians, and start the milking.

Halfway through the milking, which lasted until 14.55, Morris stormed into the parlour and marched up to the police sergeant.

'I want your name and number, Sergeant,' he cried.

The police sergeant wrote this information on a piece of paper, then Morris started crying and waving an envelope in the air.

'Now I've got to go to hospital and be x-rayed,' he shouted. 'I'll see your Chief Inspector about you.'

Morris was just about unhinged by his various misfortunes. On the farms, everything would go from bad to worse unless we took action. I could see no solution short of getting him closed down.

As soon as we finished the milking we left Valley Farm, and I set about arranging for summonses to be served on Morris. He was charged with committing seven offences under the Protection of Animals Act 1911, and appeared at a hastily arranged hearing at Aberystwyth Magistrates' Court.

The case lasted all day, through until early evening. Morris was found guilty on two of the charges and fined on each, with costs. He was also banned for life from keeping animals at Valley Farm.

Although Morris's solicitor announced that his client planned to appeal against the ban, I at last felt that some tangible progress had been made. Then, to my amazement, the Judge in the Crown Court set aside the ban. He did so reluctantly, he explained, but the Magistrates had exceeded their authority by setting a geographical limit to the original ban. If they had simply banned Morris for life from keeping animals, he would have allowed it to stand.

After that hearing I could barely speak, I was so enraged and frustrated. Once again, Morris had got off the hook, and sooner or later it would fall to me to go chasing round clearing up after his next set of misdemeanours.

Events, I am glad to say, turned out very differently. People other than me were fed up with the Morrises. Suppliers to the farm began to foreclose on him and in a mercifully short time the bailiffs arrived and animals were seized and taken away from the farm. Other livestock had to be sold to meet various debts and the fate of the farm was resolved in a way that left me with no grounds for complaint. At last, nearly three years after Morris's first warning letter, I could cross Valley Farm off my list of priority cases.

SUFFERING IN TRANSIT:
30 HOURS ON THE ROAD

Cattle wagons had been coming down from Scotland to pick up loads from markets in mid-Wales. One of these wagons was a regular at Aberystwyth market. I sent in a report about the vehicle to RSPCA Headquarters in Horsham, suggesting that we should trail it on a future run and check how the animals on board were cared for.

HQ agreed, and promised to send me an officer from their Special Investigation Unit, Inspector Frank Franzman. We were to use an unmarked car and wear civilian clothes.

On the next market day Frank and I waited in the car during the morning, my anxiety increasing as time passed and the maroon wagon failed to show up. Not until 12.15 did it arrive at the market gates. To a sigh of relief from me, the wagon made its way through the gates and drove towards the loading ramp close to the sheep pens. There it stopped, the driver got down and lowered the tailboard at the back of the vehicle. The truck had metal sides and three decks for carrying the sheep.

At 12.45 the driver started loading sheep onto his vehicle. I made a note of the time. Legally, a journey of this kind begins when the first animal is loaded. Our countdown had begun.

It took the driver 24 minutes to complete loading the sheep, and meanwhile Frank Franzman took photographs of the loading procedure. The wagon was by no means full, although there were sheep on all three decks. It looked as though the driver intended to call at other markets on the way to his final destination. At 13.09 the driver closed up the tailboard. Before he pulled away from the market, I had time to check that the registration number on the front plate matched that on the back. It did.

At 13.15 the driver eased the big wagon between the market gates. He drove through the town and joined the A487, heading south along the coast towards Aberaeron. We followed, keeping a good distance behind.

On the edge of Aberaeron, the driver forked inland onto the A482. At Lampeter, rather to my surprise, he did not stop at the cattle market but carried straight on towards Llandovery. At 14.25 he pulled into a lay-by and stayed there for 25 minutes. When he restarted his journey he continued down to the T-junction with the A40, turned left and drove into Llandovery. He reached the Cattle Mart at 15.21 and parked his vehicle.

At 16.10 he was joined by a second cattle wagon with similar markings. The driver of the second vehicle unloaded sheep into pens at the market. At 16.25 our first driver began loading more sheep onto his vehicle. Half an hour later he was ready to go. He pulled out of Llandovery and headed east on the A40. At Sennybridge, some twelve miles down the road, he stopped at a third cattle market and parked. It was now 17.20. The driver got down and walked out through the entrance to the market. From our watching car, we assumed he was going to get himself a meal before continuing his journey, presumably back to Scotland.

At 18.30 he had not reappeared. I left our car and walked over to check on the wagon. The tailboard was up. The sheep, crowded on all three decks of the vehicle, had received no food or water at any stage of their journey and nothing was available to them now.

As time went by, it became increasingly likely that the driver was going to stay overnight in Sennybridge. We were in for a cramped and uncomfortable vigil. For the rest of the evening and through the night, Frank and I took turns to watch the vehicle while the other grabbed what sleep he could. At 03.30 the market lights were suddenly switched on, flooding the yard with a harsh white light. Ten minutes later they were switched off. No-one went near the vehicle.

The driver came back to the market at 07.13. He walked round his truck, seeming more interested in the state of the wheels and tyres than in the sheep. He did not open the inspection hatches to see how they were getting on, nor did he bother to look through the ventilation slats at the side of the wagon.

At 07.19 he started the engine, but only to shift the wagon from its overnight position to a new parking space on the other side of the market. The driver went off again – no doubt for a good hot breakfast, we thought enviously – and returned an hour later. Finally, at 08.25, he climbed back into his cab and drove out of Sennybridge market. We started up and followed.

Our route continued eastwards through Brecon and then we turned north-east towards Leominster, passing through the town at ten o'clock and heading north on the A49. The driver must then have decided it was time for a cup of tea, and at 10.47 he pulled into a roadside café and stopped. Rather than risk being recognised, we drove on to the next café, bought ourselves a well-earned cuppa and sandwich and waited for our quarry to pass us. This he did at 11.15. Fifteen minutes later we were on the outskirts of Shrewsbury and half an hour later we passed through Whitchurch, still on the A49. On the open road the sheep wagon ground forward at a steady 40 mph. If we were going to Scotland, we were in for a long drive. So far, the sheep loaded in Aberystwyth had been on board, without food and water, for nearly 24 hours.

We kept to the A49, drawing closer and closer to a meeting point with the M6, the obvious fast route up to Scotland. This approach I viewed with alarm – on two counts. For one thing, I was very hungry; for another, I was getting desperate for a pee.

At 13.07 the sheep wagon turned on to the M6. I gritted my teeth. If the driver went on much longer without stopping, it was going to be the emergency toilet for me. The appointed receptacle rested on the floor behind the front seats – a luxurious two-litre plastic bottle, no less. There is little room for modesty when you trail a vehicle for the RSPCA.

For a while, though, I hung on, then hung on some more, growing increasingly desperate. Surely he must stop soon, he must be nearly as hungry as Frank and I were, quite apart from any sanitary requirements. When the next service station appeared on the signboards, we counted down the miles to it with feverish anxiety. For once, our driver did the right thing, turned off the motorway and parked. It was 13.50. Now our quarry awarded us a 20-minute break, or so it turned out, in which to speed one after the other to the Gents, refuel the car and lay in a supply of food.

We just made it on all three counts, then were off again up the M6. The next leg lasted just over two hours, then at another service station the driver made a quick seven-minute fuel stop. Off we went again, still on the M6, and then just beyond Carlisle we branched onto the A74 and crossed into Scotland at Gretna Green.

Our route continued north-west through Lockerbie, and at 17.35 the driver stopped again for ten minutes at a service station and café. Whenever we stopped, either Frank or I always kept an eye on the sheep wagon, and at no time during the journey did the driver make any kind of check on the animals he was carrying.

At Abington we forked right to the A73, driving north towards Lanark. Suddenly we took another turn and joined the A702 road to Edinburgh. I began to wonder whether we were going to end up at an east coast port, the sheep destined to suffer a long sea voyage before their lives were eventually terminated somewhere in Northern Europe, perhaps in Sweden or Denmark.

The fear was short-lived. The wagon made another sharp turn into a narrow country lane and shortly afterwards stopped at an abattoir near the town of Biggar. We pulled our car into the side of the road and watched as the maroon wagon reversed up to the unloading ramps next to the abattoir building. For the sheep it was the end of their miserable journey from mid-Wales.

It was time to make our presence known. Frank and I got out of our car and approached the driver of the wagon. We introduced ourselves. I told him the nature of the inquiries we were making and explained that we had followed him from Wales. He in turn introduced himself. His name was John Carter, he said, and he was a partner in the haulage firm that owned the wagon he had been driving.

I cautioned Mr Carter and he declined to make a statement. While I was talking to him, two other men joined us. One of them was the director of the abattoir. I explained the reason for our visit and asked if my colleague and I could see the sheep being unloaded. I also wanted to make sure that they were fed and watered.

The director of the abattoir offered his complete co-operation. He directed Mr Carter to take his vehicle round to the back of the abattoir where the sheep could be unloaded into a field. I watched them come off the wagon. Those which began their journey at Aberystwyth Cattle Mart were marked with a blue letter to identify their buyer. The last of these left the wagon at 19.00. It had been on the vehicle without food or water for 30 hours 15 minutes.

During that time, I also noted, the wagon had travelled no more than 426 miles. This meant an average rate of progress of 14.08 miles per hour. I felt the statistic only emphasised how inefficient the system was, as well as inhumane.

I told Mr Carter that I would be reporting the facts of the case, and that a prosecution might be brought against him. The director of the abattoir came over and invited Frank and myself to have a look round his establishment. Whatever his motives, it seemed reasonable to accept his offer. We went inside. It was clean, apparently well managed, one of the most up-to-date abattoirs I had seen. Nothing to find fault with there.

Frank and I went back to our car to relax, stretch out and prepare ourselves for the return journey. We were interrupted by Mr Carter. He appeared to be at the anxious-turning-contrite stage. Would we mind telling him what the requirements were of the Transit of Animals Order. He wanted to know, he said, so he could follow them properly on future journeys.

I was tired. I hoped that Mr Carter was not about to try and unblot his copybook, so to speak. What was done was done, and I was determined to report him. It would do no harm to be helpful, however, so I outlined to him the basic requirements of the Order.

As I spoke, Mr Carter may have sensed an opening, a chink of compassion that he could enlarge by impressing me with his good intentions for the future, his regrets for the past. He had not unloaded the animals at the market, he said suddenly, or fed them there, as he had not wanted to mess up the pens.

At last, I thought, for the first time in his life, it is actually getting through to him that a driver should not leave a full load of sheep locked up on his truck, without food and water, while he himself goes off for his dinner and a night's rest, returning more than 12 hours later.

I reminded Mr Carter that he was still under caution and that I would have to record anything he said. This was enough to silence him. I explained to him where he could get a copy of the regulations concerning animals in transit, and told him that our interview was over.

We set off back to Wales. It was a long journey, coming after a sleepless night, and the car helped us not at all by breaking down on the road. Next day, at last, Inspector Frank Franzman was free to return to his unit, and after some much-needed sleep I settled down to write up the case file. When it was ready, I sent it along to RSPCA Headquarters. It was up to my superiors to decide whether we had a strong enough case to bring proceedings.

Although it was the first such case the RSPCA had brought under the 1975 Order, it seemed to me that our position was strong and unambiguous. The driver, John Carter, had failed to feed the sheep in his care for a period more than double that permitted by the law.

HQ agreed, and I was instructed to go ahead and press charges. First, there was a technical matter to solve. The offence was one of a special type known as a 'continuing offence', having taken place not in one area of jurisdiction but in several, as the lorry travelled through the country. It was up to us to decide which court was the most appropriate one to hear the case.

After considering my evidence, my legal superintendent at that time suggested that the case should be heard at Brecon Magistrates' Court. He explained that Sennybridge Cattle Market fell within the Brecon Court's area, and it was there that the 12-hour period had elapsed for feeding and watering the animals.

The case was duly brought, and the charge against John Carter was as follows:

'That he being the carrier of a number of sheep being carried by road did fail to ensure that the animals were offered adequate and suitable food and wholesome water at intervals during a journey which exceeded twelve hours.

'Contrary to: Article 10(1) of the Transit of Animals (Road and Rail) Order 1975 made under the Diseases of Animals Act 1950.'

The defendant did not appear in court but sent a letter pleading guilty. This was a shrewd move since the press and television cameras were out in force that day, eager to cover the first case of its kind to be heard in court. John Carter's absence made the story a lot less newsworthy. All the same the case received, from our point of view, very satisfactory coverage on BBC and Independent Television, and also on radio.

Mr Carter was fined £100. Afterwards, a reporter from the Press Association asked me whether I was disappointed that the fine was for such a small amount. My reply was the same that day as it remained until the end of my service with the RSPCA: 'It is the conviction that matters, not the fine.'

My Superintendent was pleased with the outcome of the case. To Frank Franzman and myself he wrote: 'I heartily congratulate you both on the result of this case, which I hope will have the desired effect ... of preventing others from subjecting animals to these long journeys without rest or food.'

More than a decade later, this barbaric treatment still goes on. Cases must still be brought to court to prove the same thing – that it is cruel and thoughtless to make animals suffer in this way. Surely, by now, the point should be established. As well as bringing drivers to court, we should be looking beyond the transgressions of individuals and trying to correct the circumstances in which they happen.

APPENDIX

FOR THOSE WHO SERVE

Rather like proposing a toast, I should like to celebrate all those animals who serve humans. They do this generously and selflessly, often for their entire lives, and I think there are times when we need to remind ourselves just how much we owe these animals.

Rather than catalogue every type of serving animal that I can think of, I will concentrate on a few outstanding examples. Let their work stand for all the others.

SEARCH AND RESCUE DOG ASSOCIATION

This is a marvellous voluntary organisation which employs dogs for mountain and moorland search and rescue work. There are five centres in England, covering the Lake District, the North East, the Yorkshire Dales, the Peak District and Dartmoor. Each dog is trained to hunt for human scent carried on the wind, to trace its source, then return to the handler and lead him to the person in need, usually a climber or a rambler who has gone missing. The most popular breeds for rescue work are collies, labradors and German shepherds.

Search and Rescue teams go out in all kinds of weather and at all times of day and night. Here is the Association's summary of what happened during one recent February:

- **1 Feb 23.00 Lake District**
  13 dogs searched overnight for a geologist known to be missing whilst mapping the Skiddaw area. After an extensive search throughout the night his body was found the following afternoon by a Keswick Mountain Rescue Team (MRT) member beneath crags below Ullock Pike.
- **9 Feb 19.45 Lake District**
  5 dogs searched for a school group missing between Stake

Pass and Angle Tarn. They were found exhausted but safe north of Black Crag by a Langdale/Ambleside MRT member.

- **19 Feb 19.00 Lake District**
  1 dog was called to search for a climber believed missing on Great End. He was found walking down near Burnthwaite by a Search Dog and Handler.
- **24 Feb 00.30 Lake District**
  14 dogs on the Annual Reassessment Course searched areas around the Honister and Newlands passes for a missing boy. After an overnight search he was found safe near Red Pike by a Search Dog and Handler.
- **26 Feb 23.30 Peak District**
  5 dogs searched overnight areas on Kinder plateau for a missing man. He was found safe next morning at Fairbrook Naze by a Search Dog and Handler.
- **28 Feb 07.30 North East**
  1 dog was called to search for a missing man thought to be in a depressed condition. The search was called off when his body was found by police near Goathland.

Altogether that year, police and Mountain Rescue Teams called out SARDA on 63 occasions, involving 245 individual dog turnouts. They made 11 important casualty finds and cleared many large areas during major searches.

The dogs also take part in disaster operations. Teams went abroad for the first time in 1986 to assist in the El Salvador earthquake tragedy. Two years later they were at Lockerbie after a sabotaged PanAm jumbo jet crashed on the town in the Scottish Borders killing all 259 passengers and 11 people on the ground. Wreckage was scattered for miles, bodies lay everywhere in the town and nearby fields, many of them badly mutilated. Fragments of metal littered streets and gardens, and one of the aircraft's wings gouged a huge crater destroying half a dozen houses.

The SARDA dogs and their handlers were magnificent, carrying on despite injuries to the dogs' legs and paws caused by sharp metal debris. They worked untiringly to try and locate bodies trapped in the wrecked town, sniffing out clues and collecting evidence for the police inquirers.

One image of them stays with me to this day. A handler and his

dog were standing near a mobile canteen. The handler had just got
himself a Mars bar. He was clearly upset by some of the things he
had seen that day. Somehow, so close is the relationship between
a handler and his dog that the man's sadness had transmitted itself
to the dog. They shared the Mars bar, the dog looked up at his
handler and I had an overwhelming sense of the pure comradeship
that bound them together. Tired and not a little miserable, they had
seen what they had seen, and now were grateful for a moment's
rest, taken, as always, together.

Some while later, I was delighted to meet SARDA members at
a special gathering. The Leeds branch of RSPCA then made them
a donation and its national HQ gave them an award for their work
at Lockerbie. I was thrilled for them. I knew that some of the dogs
had received injuries and I was so pleased that their contribution
was being recognised. Sometimes we see dogs go into action on our
behalf, particularly police dogs, and we forget that they too face
danger, just as much as their handler, and may be hurt or even
killed.

What really impresses me about this kind of serving dog is the
consistency and reliability of their work. Wherever they are
needed, they are there. You may not always see them, but you can
be sure they are not far away.

Not long ago I was at the Queen Mother's Ninetieth Birthday
parade in London. I arrived early, while police dogs and their
handlers were still busy checking the Underground stations, the
sewers and many big public buildings along the route – all to make
it a safe place for the crowds of wellwishers who were pouring into
that part of the city.

During the parade itself, as the Queen Mother drove past, I
happened to look up onto the roof of the building opposite, in
Horse Guard's Parade. There stood a policeman and his dog, still
watching, still looking after us. They remained at their post until
the day was over, and the crowd finally dispersed. How many of
those people would be aware, I wondered, that they owed the
success of their day in some modest part to the contribution of those
patient animals?

'PAT' DOGS

One of the most relaxing things I know is to stroke a cat. No matter what may be churning about in my mind after a hectic or worrying day, if I sit down in an easy chair at home, with Landy our marmalade cat by my side, and he is happy to sit there and let me stroke him, the effect is so soothing it calms me down and brings me back to normal quicker than anything I know. It is as though my tensions are massaged away as I stroke his fur. If I had a sense of isolation, that too dissolves because now I have his company.

Doctors, psychologists and charity workers are realising more and more that animals can play an important therapeutic role, especially with the elderly, children without families and people who are mentally disturbed. This idea lay behind the 'PAT' Dog visiting scheme, founded in 1983 by Lesley Scott Ordish. She explains:

'Many people have to give up much-loved pets to enter institutions. This can cause distress and even lead to severe depression. Early on we found patients who had become withdrawn and would not speak to staff or other residents. When the dogs started coming, their attitudes changed. We could see that the dogs did more than just provide an enjoyable visit, a break in the daily routine. They actually got people talking again.

'To begin with, the dog arrives and the patient begins to stroke it. If he or she likes dogs, it's the most natural thing in the world to do. Gradually, stresses are reduced, their feeling of isolation leaves them and they want to start talking to us, usually about their memories.'

The handler, of course, is an important part of the team. He or she is the speaking contact, the one the patient turns to next for company and conversation.

The 'PAT' Dogs scheme was launched through PRO Dogs, a national charity. Its name stands for PRO-Dogs Active Therapy, and today more than 5,000 dogs of many different breeds have passed the organisers' temperament test and gone into service. Golden retrievers seem to make the most amiable visitors, but there are also Irish wolfhounds, Bernese mountain dogs, English setters, German shepherds, Border collies, and numerous other pedigree and cross-bred dogs.

Quietly and gently, they do a wonderful job. Outside the scheme, I don't think the work of these dogs is given much attention. If you can, spare a thought for them next time you go to visit someone in hospital or in a residential home.

FRIENDS IN WHITE HARNESS

More familiar, because we see them out and about in our streets and on the buses, are the Guide Dogs for the Blind. In their white harness, these patient, almost saintly animals perform a unique service in helping the unsighted and the partly sighted to lead an independent life.

Without their guide dog, these people would be so much more restricted, in some cases virtual prisoners in their home. Unable to do their own shopping, they would be reliant on others to help them out and do these and other jobs for them. Thanks to the guide dog, the blind person can be as liberated as he or she can manage to be. That is a wonderful gift, and we can all of us be grateful to these dogs.

It is important to remember, too, that the idea of animals in service is entirely of our own making. We, the humans, view it as a good idea and then seek to impose it on a particular group of animals, turning them into guide dogs, mountain rescue dogs, police horses and so on. The animal, as ever, has no choice in its future role. Provided it is the right type, has the right temperament and responds well in training, into service it will go. For dogs and horses there are no buy-out options. They cannot turn round and say, 'Sorry, this isn't really for me. I resign.'

Of all the animals in service, perhaps it is the guide dog which has to make the biggest sacrifices. Unlike a police horse, for example, which gets a good gallop every now and then, the guide dog has to make do with little exercise and little chance to relax. It is on duty for the rest of its working life.

Its specialised training goes against its natural instincts. It has to walk slowly and soberly at all times, keeping to a pace set by its owner. All dogs love to rush about and hunt for smells, but the guide dog is trained to restrain itself and ignore them.

The well-trained dog accepts this. Those that I have seen bear up very well to these restrictions. However, not all owners are as patient as they might be, and this can lead to difficulties.

Although it may be an unpopular thing to say, blind or partly sighted people are not necessarily animal lovers. Why should they be? Not all sighted people are animal lovers, either. From time to time, a guide dog is acquired by someone who is not fully sympathetic to the animal's needs.

I had a case where a blind woman flew into a temper and started kicking her guide dog. They were in a market at the time, and the poor dog had been unable to resist all the tantalising smells coming from the food counters. It started sniffing about, and dearly would have liked to nip off and investigate these wonders at close quarters.

Of course, it should not have done this; nor even have been tempted to sniff about. But guide dogs are dogs, after all. What it most needed was an understanding owner who would have recognised the problem and had the patience and sense to take the dog out of the market and into the everyday, unexciting atmosphere of the street. Unfortunately, the woman lost her temper and took her anger out on the dog.

At such times it is embarrassing, and counter-productive, for a bystander or someone such as myself to step in with a reprimand. People would say, 'Go on, leave her alone. Can't you see she's blind,' and the situation would be made worse rather than defused.

A more diplomatic solution would be for all Guide Dogs for the Blind to carry a disc on their harness which bore a special number for that dog. Anyone who felt that further action was necessary could then report the incident to the Association, giving them the number of the dog, and it would be up to the Association to deal with the owner as it saw fit.

On the credit side, I feel that the guide dog scheme does much excellent work. I have come across many dog-human partnerships which obviously are successful. The pair are devoted to each other and share their lives in the most heartwarming way.

Snowy is a good example. I know about Snowy because she was one of ours – in her young days she was taken into the RSPCA Animal Home in Leeds because no-one wanted her. A placid, good-natured German shepherd cross-bred bitch, aged about 13 months, she faced a doubtful future until we had a visit from two officials from the guide dogs training centre in Middlesbrough.

They chose Snowy as a suitable candidate for training, and away she went to Middlesbrough. For some long while I heard nothing more about her, which is not surprising, given the hundreds and thousands of dogs passing through the Animal Home. Then, by chance, I found out that Snowy had passed through her training course at the Guide Dogs Centre and was now acting as the eyes for Helen, a young lady living in Rotherham.

I telephoned Helen and she was happy to tell me about their life together. She worked as an audio typist in Sheffield, and each day Snowy took her into work, by train and bus, and brought her home each evening. Helen's great hobby was singing, and she was a member of the Sheffield Philharmonic. Naturally, whenever she went to choir practice or to perform in a concert, Snowy went too.

She told me that Snowy had even become part of the concert team. When the conductor asked the choir to stand, Snowy stood up with them. Helen was delighted with her German shepherd friend and companion. They had been together for eight years when I spoke to her, and looked forward to many more years together. It sounded as though they had an ideal partnership - the caring owner and her dedicated dog.

HORSE REPORT

Learning to ride horse can be both satisfactory and at times painful. When I see a young person learning to ride, I allow myself a quiet smile as I remember the poem sent to me by Mrs P. Mason of Leeds which I would like to share with you.

You have to be an athlete if you want to ride a horse –
I learned this painful lesson when I took a Riding Course.
Put your left foot in the stirrup, the riding mistress said –
Unfortunately, I cannot get my foot above my head.
The animal they gave me, looked to be ten feet tall,
The only way I'd mount him was standing on a wall.
Now point your toes forward and keep your heels low down,
Head up, back straight and elbows in, she informed me with a
* frown.*
Hold your reins less firmly and don't slump in your seat –

We'd only done ten minutes, yet I was feeling beat.
She tried to teach me how to trot and how to turn him round,
The only thing I really learned was how to hit the ground.
You've got to show him who's the boss, she said in tones so grim –
My horse had worked that out for himself, he knew that it was him.
At last the session ended and I went home stiff and sore
Vowing that I wouldn't go near horses any more
I gave it everything I had, now I'm only half alive.
Next time I want to ride around, I think I'll learn to drive!

We, and our ancestors, owe more to the horse than we can possibly imagine. How pleasant it is that, long since the need has passed for horses to serve as our most important draught and riding animal, we have preserved the breeds and found useful things for them to do.

One of the most worthwhile organisations is Riding for the Disabled. Their ponies give disabled children and adults that special contact with animals which they might so easily miss. The relationship between horse and rider builds an important trust, and the disabled rider must feel a marvellous sense of achievement through being able to sit on a horse and feel it move beneath them.

All pony and horse people enthuse about the tremendous bond of friendship which grows up between them and the animal. That sense of relying on each other – the horse to give its owner a gentle and reassuring ride (or an exhilarating gallop if that is what he wants) – and the rider undertaking to guide the horse firmly and accurately, and not force it beyond its natural capacities.

There have been many books written by able-bodied riders – children's novels, the life stories of jockeys, trainers, showjumpers and eventers, and many others. I would like to know more about how disabled riders feel. It seems to me that they could have something of enormous value to tell us, about disabled people as a group, their needs and how we might experiment with other ways to help them.

Riding a pony, for someone who could not under ordinary circumstances mount the animal, or control it without external guidance or special equipment, must be such a singular experience. Through it the rider can learn so much – about companionship and teamwork on all sorts of levels, about balance and dignity, and that amazing positive surge we all feel when we have achieved something that we may have thought was beyond us.

I hope more disabled riders will be encouraged to tell us about their experiences, and that others will take up the research on their behalf.

Earlier, I mentioned our ancestors and the world in which they lived, dependent at every turn on horses to pull their wagons to market and their stagecoaches on long journeys, as well as their ploughs in the fields.

The heavy horse is still a breed to wonder at, and I am delighted that so many are still around and flourishing. Nowadays they pull brewers' drays, all decked out with bright colours and a uniformed drayman in the driving seat. You see them still on working farms, at county shows and on ceremonial occasions. People love them – and for a special reason. Those giant horses – the Shires and the Clydesdales, and the French Percherons – remind us of our past and can tell us also a little of what it was like in the 'Good Old Days'.

I had a brilliant experience of this. Pulled by two Shire horses from Leeds, I rode in an open-topped charabanc through the streets of Middlesbrough. We jolted along over cobblestones at one stage, and the whole journey went at a leisurely pace. There was no rush, the great horses clipped and clopped and clonked along until we got there. No speeding, no petrol fumes, and on that day, no traffic jams. I felt it was another world – all thanks to those two horses.

CATS IN INDUSTRY

You will have heard, I am sure, of office cats and factory cats. T.S. Eliot certainly knew about them. In *Old Possum's Book of Practical Cats* he introduced a formidable range of eccentrics, among them Bustopher Jones the spat-wearing Clubland Cat, and Skimbleshanks the Railway Cat. No-one knows where they come from. One day there they are, watching over the Post Office sorting room, or sitting on the factory floor with a mouse in their jaws.

Naturally, for this and other services, the factory people are happy to feed their new feline caretaker, and even lay down bedding for him or her in some warm corner of the building. The weeks go by and the cat seems to have been there forever, until the factory is due to shut down for its annual holiday. Crisis! What's going to happen to (*whisper*) 'him in the corner'?

Now, luckily, all that is taken care of. Just lift up the 'phone and call Cats in Industry. This charity devotes itself to cats which have occupied offices and factories. When everyone else is away, they go in and make sure the cats are fed and watered and kept in good health. They will also place a cat if someone has a building that needs taking care of, usually because of mice and rats.

Not all cats are layabouts, as some would maintain. Far from it. In fact, I think those factory cats have been very clever. It cannot be easy for an animal to come to an informal, unwritten agreement with a company of humans, whereby it fixes itself up with free food and lodging in exchange for an unspecified spot of ratting, preferably at night so as not to upset the workers.

The skill of these cats deserves wider recognition, and I am glad that Cats in Industry is around to offer support and encouragement.

AND FINALLY, COWS AND SHEEP

We have a strange attitude in this country. If a horse becomes old, and there is talk of killing it off or selling it for meat probably abroad, say to France or Belgium where they enjoy eating horsemeat – there is a public outcry. 'No, no!' everybody cries. 'Poor old horse. Put him out to grass, he deserves a few years of retirement before he goes.'

No-one ever says that about a cow. For years and years a cow provides us with milk and a succession of calves. But then, when she becomes barren and can produce no more milk, she is sent away for slaughter. No-one raises a voice in protest, or thinks for a moment that this cow has served her masters well and should be put out to grass in recognition of her work.

It puzzles me that there is this way of thinking. If a horse is worth all that fuss and attention, why not a cow?

We operate a double standard, and without doubt it is connected to our meat-eating habits. To those of us – the great majority of the population – who want to eat meat, it is convenient to relegate the main food animals – the pig, hen, cow and sheep – to a more lowly position, beneath the usual norms of consideration. Having done so, we can then eat them with a clear conscience.

This helps to explain our more exalted regard for the horse, and other farm animals which in this country are generally viewed as less appetising. The goat is another example. We grant these a higher place in the social ranking of animals so that when they grow old, we retire them to a field rather than send them to the abattoir.

With regional variations, influenced by local tastes for this or that animal, these systems of social ranking occur throughout the world. They are influenced also by prevailing religions and philosophies, and are very old indeed.

For centuries, philosophers, scientists and religious thinkers have argued over the rights and wrongs of eating animal flesh. In time the debate gave rise to a strong vegetarian movement, which in Britain dates from about 1790. Today, we live in a utilitarian society. Religion has lost its power and most people, when they think about it, can justify killing animals for food provided the animals are well looked after during their lifetime and then slaughtered as humanely as possible.

There is still a strong vegetarian movement, and in the last twenty years it has become increasingly vocal and important. More and more people are deserting the butcher's counter – even if they still allow themselves to eat fish and poultry.

Whether the vegetarian view will entirely prevail, I cannot say. I am fairly sure it is an issue that will not be resolved in my lifetime. But I am *very* interested in the way our attitudes towards farm animals are being changed by the advance of vegetarianism. If it means a better deal even for some of our cows, pigs, sheep and hens, I am all for it.

In the end, I think it comes down to this. If we breed these animals, we are responsible for their existence. Therefore, we should try to find more ways to give them a better life. That, surely, is their right.

AUTHOR'S

ACKNOWLEDGEMENTS

There are also many people who have played an important part in making this book possible, and I would particularly like to thank the following: former colleagues in the RSPCA, especially the management and staff of the Leeds branch; the West Yorkshire Police; the *Yorkshire Evening Post* (and in particular Bruce Smith, and Richard Taylor – now with the BBC); veterinary surgeons, and all others who have helped the cause of animal welfare.

I am also grateful to Peter Singer for his book *Animal Liberation* (Thorsons, 2nd ed 1991) which was the source of much of the information on pages 13-16.

Finally, I would like to thank my wife Susan for her constant support over the years.